Praise from Ar
The Little Bo

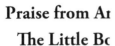

It is encouraging to find an author who, sensitive to our times, presents a positive future. We all need to read this book!

Grady Harp

Love this...[in us] exists the keys to greatness. Powerful read.

Ben

One of the great things about this story is the simplicity. However the greatest thing about this book is its practicality.

Kevin Wilson

Great motivational book...Definitely would recommend.

Maryna Aloshyna

I absolutely loved this book! The book is a beautiful reminder of the wisdoms of living your best life...The book is honestly a classic and serves as a helpful tool on how to navigate a successful, giving, purpose driven life.

Mendi

...most people will relate to [it]...precise guidance to help the reader cut through the noise and to discover their purpose and pursue it.

AmazonLover

Well-written parable for those on the spiritual or self-improvement path...well written and easy to read, while poetic and even inspirational...this book reminds me the most of The Alchemist, by Paulo Coelho...

Diane NH

Eloquently enunciated story that unfolds itself through a gripping tale...soulful and riveting book that can be read again.

Pat Mitchell

I like how the story was embedded with lessons...much more relevant and meaningful.

Suzy Kelly

Excellent, powerful, concise guide to bringing out the best, truest parts of you. Highly recommend the book and author.

TZ

...powerful message...delivered with great candor and truth.

Martez Andrews II

Great little motivational book.

Tim Bohr

...an inspirational book with a great message...full of hope and motivates the reader to grab life with both hands. Highly recommend.

Silvie

I enjoyed reading this book. It holds a lot of truth and is written in an engaging way. I believe all readers...will enjoy this read.

A. Christensen

...found this similar to Robin Sharma - a mix of personal development with a modern parable.

lzblz548

Praise for Ari Gunzburg and the 5 Keys To Greatness

"It really kind of touched a spot for me, in terms of focusing on my inner self and how I can be in charge of my destiny."

Dante Jofferion, a Director at Cushman & Wakefield

"Every time, he brought a passion and fire. He's an impactful speaker who I take pleasure in highly recommending."

Jake Rosenberg, Host of The Power Entrepreneur

"...Ari's thoughts on positivity and on the way you look at life and on the way you present yourself in a positive way...means a lot to me based on things I've gone through in my own life."

Mark Adkins at the National Eye Institute at NIH

"Ari is an overall great public speaker. He speaks with poise and confidence. He had no problem capturing the attention of more than 50 colleagues when he came to speak at my workplace. Would definitely recommend."

Ross Filo, Capital Analyst at Nestlé

"We invited Ari here today to talk about change within our organization . . . Ari was point-on with his message, and it is certainly one that will carry forward for as we enter into our new healthcare journey. Thanks Ari, it was a great experience, and we look forward to drawing on some of the important points that you brought forward to us today."

Lisa Voll-Lego, Executive Director of Thresholds Homes & Supports

"Ari is a master story teller. He engaged all our senses during the presentation...His presentation was inspiring and motivating. He gave step-by-step and actionable information for the audience to take away to change their life. Thank you Ari!!"

Michael Wigglesworth, Project Manager at MNCPPC

"What an OUTSTANDING keynote speaker!!! Ari inspires audiences to take action and make a difference in this world. This is truly his gift."

Lisa Newburger, CEO of Discuss Directives

"It was a great presentation from Ari, he was very personable and engaging with our customers and our guests who were there. It was a comfortable speech that was easy to listen to.

Everybody loves a story, and you love when you can connect it back to your organization, and I think Ari did a great job of doing that for us."

Jamie Carr, IREM Association Executive

"...the feedback from the men attending the event was positive and they felt that he had done a good job also. This is a maximum security prison and not your typical audience. They were attentive and engaged in what he had to say."

Susan Cowan, Activities at State Correctional Facility in PA

"Moving, thought provoking presentation - loved it. Ari presented to a professional group and he was inspiring...relatable to both professional or private life situations."

Brenda Watson, MDHIMA

the little book of
GREATNESS

a parable about unlocking your destiny

Using the 5 Keys To Greatness to Unlock Your Destiny,
Achieve Your Dreams, and Live Your Best Life.

ARI GUNZBURG

Cover design by Ari Gunzburg

Published by MindSpark in Cleveland, Ohio.
mindsparkmotivation.com

To learn more about Ari Gunzburg, please visit arigunz.com

To my wife. With all my love, for forever and a day.

-Ari

TABLE OF CONTENTS

"To live is to choose. But to choose well, you must know who you are and what you stand for, where you want to go and why you want to go there."

-Kofi Annan

Introduction

I N TOTAL DARKNESS, it only takes a little light to shine the way. In a world where so many are in darkness of one type or another, we can shine a little light for each other, so we can all see the way, the way to our own greatness.

We each have the potential of greatness within us. A greatness of our own understanding. We often lack the tools to refine this greatness and bring us to our destiny. There are many books and programs on the subject of hyper-achievement. But there seem to be few books that give the strength and the tools to unlock your destiny, achieve your dreams and live your best life.

The 5 Keys To Greatness is a simple, easy-to-remember framework. The 5 Keys can be applied in many different ways, to all different lives. If you explore these concepts you may find unexpected depth. Keep exploring these concepts and if you want, fit other systems into the 5 Keys.

The entire system can be summarized in a few short paragraphs. I hope you find the story impactful, though, so I am leaving this overview for after the story.

I recommend you wait to implement the keys until after you read the story and know all 5 Keys. If you take notes or journal as you travel through the story, you will see more ways the keys can impact your life.

Above all, remember your greatness within. Let it out, let it into the world. Believe in yourself and in what you are doing. With enough of us following the 5 Keys, living our destiny, we will change the world.

The 5 Keys To Greatness is a framework for you to use in your own private way, in your own private life. I am continuing to develop these ideas, hoping to revolutionize the way we interact. Please, let's stay in touch.

Let's keep shining that light for each other.

Baltimore, Maryland
July 6, 2020

01

Troubled at the Cliffs

T HE MAN STOOD on the cliff, watching the cars speed past below. He thought of the world as it is, while watching the headlights zip by. The day was turning to night, with a breeze in the air. The man shivered, pulling his coat tighter. The beauty of the fall colors adorned the trees all around. He couldn't see the fireworks, the colors, because he stood lost in thought.

The man felt troubled; troubled about the world, troubled about his life, troubled about his place in the grand scheme of things. He had so many unanswered questions, so many things left unsaid.

Unaccomplished goals haunted him day and night. These goals only haunted him when he had time to think–which, he recognized, he didn't have a lot of time to do. He pulled out his phone to check messages, flipped through notifications, put his phone away . . . what was he thinking of again?

The man heard rustling in the woods behind him. It was not yet night, so he turned to see what was making the commotion. Now the rustling noise became more of a step, step sound. The man peered into the woods, trying to see who, or what, was approaching.

"Hey there!" a voice rang out in the dusk.

"Hello?" the man said, trying to see, as a figure emerged from the shadows of the trees.

"Hiya!" An older, distinguished-looking gentleman with white hair and a long dark coat stood in front of the man. "Whatchya doing out here?"

The man stood, regarding the newcomer. "Thinking."

"About what?"

The man took a deep breath, and turned to watch the cars again. "Life."

The old man stood, watching him. They were silent for a while. "Care to tell me about it?"

The man on the cliff took a deep breath. He put his hands on his hips, before covering his face. He dropped his hands, then turned toward the old man. "Can't a guy wallow in peace?"

"You seem troubled. I wanted to know if you wanted to talk about it."

"DAMMIT!!" The man lowered himself to the ground, feet hanging over the edge. The man put his hands to his eyes, and shook as sobs racked his body.

The older man slowly, carefully, settled down on the ground beside him. He put a hand on the man's back briefly, then put his hand down and sat quietly.

The daylight disappeared. The lights on the cars below flashed past, yellow in one direction, red in the other. The whooshing of cars flying down the highway filled the air. The only other sounds were the insects with their forest symphony, and the muffled sound of crying.

The older man simply sat.

Eventually the sobbing subsided. The man looked around, seeing the older gentleman still sitting there. "What do you want?!"

The older man smiled and looked at him. "Who says I want anything?"

"Everyone wants something nowadays." The man exhaled sharply. "Though it doesn't seem to be money so much anymore."

"What do you mean by that?"

"I mean that less and less it seems like they want my money. More and more it seems like they want my mind and my attention."

The old man laughed. "Only your mind and complete attention?! That doesn't seem to be asking for much."

The younger man grinned, chuckled a little. "No, it used to seem like they wanted my money any way I could give it. Sales, telemarketers, restaurants, toys, gadgets, whatever. Now I get sucked into my phone, my computer, my tablet, everything. Then I find that as much as these devices should be saving my time, they are wasting my time. Digital devices make it that much harder to feel productive."

The older man looked around at the woods behind them, gesturing at it all. "And this doesn't help?"

The younger man laughed. "I haven't been out here in twenty years. Don't have the time anymore."

"Have you considered that you simply don't make the time?"

The man laughed. "Fine. That may be true. I still have a hard time with things."

"I get the picture; at least a little bit. That much is for sure." The older man sighed. "You know, you aren't the first person having difficulty with the new world order."

The younger man threw up his arms. "Difficulty? What the hell do you know of difficulty? You think I'm up here to hang out? Catch a minute? Ugh!" He stood up, walked back toward the woods, while the older man turned his body to better see. He put his hands on his head, flipped around, then walked over and confronted the man again. "I've had enough!! Enough! Nothing makes sense anymore. People have gone completely crazy–completely disconnected from reality! Everyone is running after the next greatest thing–not realizing that it's not helping. I'd bet if someone did a study, they would find a correlation between dissatisfaction in life and the advent of smartphones! Maybe they already have!"

"Do you think that smartphones are the problem?"

The younger man stopped, looked at him, shrugged. "No . . . I mean yes . . . I mean–I don't know. They're definitely not part of the solution. Smartphones are not helping anything. But it is more than that. I . . . I see things that make me wonder what the hell we were thinking when we signed up for this stuff. People talk about how cool it is, how helpful it is, but they are worse and worse off all the time."

"Smartphones. We were talking of smartphones."

"No. I don't think smartphones are the problem. Or at least, not the whole problem. Maybe it's a symptom of a larger problem."

The old man chuckled. "Smartphones might be the problem. But let's say for a moment they're not. What do you think is the problem? What do you think brought you up here, to, ah, figure out what comes next?"

The younger man looked at the older man. He saw the kindness in his eyes, caring, empathy. He saw the wrinkles of wisdom around his face, the smile that reached deep into his eyes. And in that moment, he made a decision.

The younger man sat on a large rock. He sighed. "Yeah. Yeah, you're right. I don't know if I fully knew it myself. But yeah, I may have come up here because ... because ... I don't know ...

"I ... I don't know. Nothing makes sense anymore. The world that made sense only a few years ago, it's different. I can't explain it. I can't define it. I only know that it feels different than it did, and far more overwhelming. I don't know if I'm coming or going. I'm on social media because it's supposed to be helpful, but half the time I go online and wonder what the hell I just did with my time. It always seems like there is one more thing to do, one more article to read. And for what?! It doesn't help me ... at all.

"I don't know what to do anymore. My life feels out of control, I don't feel like I know what to focus on. I used to have clarity, and then the days, the years went by and I feel like I've lost my clarity, lost my focus.

"All I truly understand is that I am overwhelmed. I feel like I'm at the end of my rope. Ahh!" The younger man walked back to the edge of the cliff, breathed out loudly. "Help! There! I said it! Help." He sat down again, feet over the cliff, back next to the older man. "I . . . I don't know what to do . . . I don't know how to bring my life back to some level of normalcy."

"Would you believe me if I told you I've been through the exact same thing?" The older man stood with some difficulty. He watched the cars, and the younger man, while standing on the edge.

The younger man turned to look up. "How the hell is that possible!? The smartphone? The social media?"

The older man chuckled and raised his hands. "Okay, not 'exactly' exactly. But really, really close. I've been through feelings like this: feelings of inadequacy, feeling overwhelmed, not knowing the steps to take to move forward. I've also contemplated what it's all for in similar, ah, precarious situations." The old man gestured to the cliff and the cars racing by below.

"And!? What did you do?!"

The old man smiled. "I jumped."

"You jumped?" The younger man stood back up, facing the old man.

"Yes. I jumped. I took the biggest leap of faith of my life, and started to trust in the process a little more."

"What do you mean? What process?"

"It's a bit hard to explain all at once, or even in one sitting. I actually have people who explain it far better than I can; I call them keyholders. If you can wait a few days or so, and talk to everyone, you'll see it will all be worth it."

The younger man stood still, watching him. They stood, silently, for a few minutes.

"Worth it? Says who?"

"Every person I've helped in the past. Look, you have nothing to lose by listening to me, and everything to gain. And don't worry, this cliff isn't going anywhere. All that I ask is that you follow through, that you hear everything they have to say."

"Why should I trust you at all?"

"Because deep in your heart you know you want to. I was right here, in the same type of mood, many years ago. And someone came up the trail behind me, just like I did now to you. He taught me this secret, the 5 Keys to Greatness. Now I want to share it with you."

"What's so good about it?"

"Well. To start with, I know many people who went from the brink of despair to the edge of greatness. And now, as they unlock their own individual greatness, they are helping others."

"Helping others? How?"

"Tell you what. Why don't we start off by heading down together, I'll tell you a bit more about it. Tomorrow, you can visit one of my friends, hear her perspective on it. She'll even send you to the rest of the keyholders, so you can learn each key. You don't need to take my word for it."

The younger man thought about it. "What do you want from me?"

"Only a little time. Time you will regain in great abundance as you put this framework into practice. If you find it valuable, you can share it with others too. Can you do that?"

The younger man thought for a while. He thought of everything going wrong in his life. He thought of everything going wrong around the world. He said, "And if I don't find it valuable?"

"Continue your life as you see fit. You're on your own at that point. But I think you'll find it worthwhile."

"Okay. Fair enough. What's your name, anyway?"

The older man smiled. "My name isn't that important. But you can call me Pinch."

"I'm David."

The two walked down together, stumbling through the darkness while making their way back to the parking lot. On the way down, the older man told David to write down what he thought were the five most fundamental elements to a good life. Once finished, David would go visit a bartender named Regina.

02

Vantage Point

D AVID AWOKE EARLY the next day. He sat in the early morning hours with a notebook and a pencil to brainstorm. And he worked on the list from the older man.

Later that day, after work and dinner, David went to the restaurant, Vantage Point, to visit Regina. He noted the flat-roofed building, with bright neon lights on the roof. It was in a trendy, hip part of town. People stood inside and out, but it wasn't over-crowded.

David walked in, looking through the crowd. He noticed the people having a good time, noticed the decor. Decor consisting of memorabilia and photos showing different vantage points in nature, including the Grand Canyon, Cloud's Rest, Everest, Matterhorn, and more.

David walked to the bar and sat down. A short dark bartender, a lady with short purple hair, walked over to him. David wondered if it was Regina. He asked for a beer.

"Here ya go!" She smiled at him and started moving on.

"Hang on!" David leaned over the bar and called to her, "Is there a Regina who works here?"

The lady stopped what she was doing and tilted her head to the side as she grabbed a better look at David. With his button down shirt and jacket askew, she wondered why he asked for Regina.

"Who wants to know?"

David smiled a little. "I do. My name is David. I was sent here to talk to Regina. About some 5 Keys To Greatness thing."

The lady laughed. "Why didn't you say so? I'm Regina. Hang on."

Regina walked around the bar, found the other bartenders, and whispered to them. They waved to David. The restaurant and bar areas were both comfortably busy. Being after dinnertime, but before the witching hour, the bartender and servers weren't overwhelmed.

Regina came back to David and said, "Come on."

David jumped up with his beer, and the two of them walked toward the bathroom area. "Where are we going?" David asked.

Regina responded by waving him on to follow her. Her gray tank top and green pants contrasted her dark skin.

In the hallway, past the bathrooms, in a small alcove, Regina pulled down a sweatshirt from a set of hooks on the wall. She opened a door which blended almost perfectly into the wall, revealing narrow, steep stairs reminiscent of European architecture. Regina stepped in and started up the stairs, calling behind her to close the door.

David pulled the door shut behind him and started up the stairs, holding on to the railing. He followed Regina, past a doorway on the first landing, continuing up the stairs. At the top of the stairs was an exit door. Regina put her shoulder into the door to push it open, revealing the roof.

David looked around at the bright neon bar sign, at the seventies-era patio set sitting on a deck made of pallets on the flat roof. They walked to the chairs and sat down.

"Okay!" Regina smiled. "That's better. I love this place, but sometimes I can't hear myself think. If we are going to have a real conversation, we need to be able to think." The music and muted sounds of conversation were now background noise, drifting out of the building and floating up to their ears.

David fidgeted in his seat, put his beer down on the table.

Regina asked, "You said you were sent over to talk to me. Who sent you?"

"An older man. Pinch. He told me to write down what I think are the five essential things to leading a good life, and then to come see you."

Regina blinked, surprised. "You saw Pinch? Actually?"

David nodded.

"Hmm." Regina continued to regard him. "What five things did you write down?"

David felt around his jacket, looking. He found the paper, pulled it out.

"Here it is. I wrote down a few more than five things, I kind of brainstormed it out, you know?"

Regina nodded.

"Let's see. Family, that's important to a good life. Hard work. Good luck, like being in the right place at the right time."

Regina smiled and nodded again. "Go on."

"Learning. Life long learning. Stability. Good self-esteem. That's about all I came up with. I mean, there are other things on here, but they're pretty similar."

Regina nodded again. "That is a great list. Good start. I want to point out something about these things. What you wrote down is definitely true, but they are limiting. Think about it.

"Family is important, of course. But there are people without family, for whom a good life is definitely possible. What if we changed this to be more about being present in the present moment? Now family fits into the larger category, but a lot of other things fit in as well."

David thought about this, nodding his head as he saw how it fit in.

"Hard work is important, but also can be better placed in a broader category. What if we changed this to be more about persistence and tenacity? Now hard work is a part of the category, but so is continuing forward in the face of all adversity."

David again nodded.

Regina said, "It's the same with the other items on your list. Stability is a part of working to improve yourself by focusing on the positive and remaining persistent. You gain stability when you stay the course. When you are always growing, always learning. And self-esteem is influenced by looking at yourself in a more positive way.

"Learning," Regina laughed, "you are right about

learning. But it's so obvious it doesn't need to be categorized."

She leaned over to a cooler by the table, pulled out a drink and opened it. "Humans are growth oriented. When we are not learning, we are not growing, and when we are not growing, we are stagnating. The more we focus on growing, on being better today than we were yesterday, the better off we become.

"You also brought up good luck. Most people don't realize that people who seem to have good luck often create it for themselves. They create it by focusing on the positive.

"Good luck comes from being in tune with what you desire, in tune with your destiny. It has to do with how the subconscious mind filters out millions of bits of data, only allowing a little information through to the conscious mind. So you focus on whatever confirms what you already believe. You'll probably cover this later, during the fourth key. In a nutshell, your beliefs can literally change your experience. This means good luck is often created by the person experiencing it.

Regina laughed. "Sorry! You mentioned good luck and I wanted to point this out." She laughed again, subdued. "This is one of my demons." She sighed. "David, I don't like to tell people this, but it's important." Regina took a deep breath. Her resolve could be viewed in the set of her shoulders, the stubborn tilt of her chin.

"I thought that if I could just have some good luck, everything would be okay. My life got deeper and deeper into what felt like bad luck. It felt like nothing was working. I got more and more depressed, as I continued to see my entire life falling apart around me.

"I was introduced to the 5 Keys To Greatness by a lady named Yolanda. At that point, I was completely and totally miserable. I thought that bad luck was my lot in life." Regina held out her thumb and forefinger, pinched to a small point. "I was this close to being evicted, my car was dead, I lost my job, and my family, little though it was, wasn't talking to me. Everything was going wrong. It was one problem after another. And I thought it was everyone else's fault.

"This lady Yolanda, she probably saved my life. She showed me how I could take control of my life and how my thoughts directly affect the things around me. She taught me about taking responsibility for my actions. She told me about the 5 Keys To Greatness. She explained that I could elevate my entire life and create a life better than I ever thought possible."

David looked at Regina. He took a sip. "Pinch also went on about greatness." David sighed. "But greatness? I'm just trying to survive. I don't know that I'm interested in greatness."

Regina laughed. "Well, what do you think greatness means? Not to the world . . . to you."

"Hmm." David thought for a moment. "I think greatness to the world means so much. It could mean being selfless, like maybe Gandhi or Mother Theresa. Maybe it could mean famous rockstars, or actors, or something. People who make a big difference in the world."

Regina nodded. "Yes, that's what greatness means to everyone else. What does it mean to YOU? Specifically to you, not to the world."

"To me . . ." David pursed his eyebrows. "I don't know . . . maybe being more than I am. Being amazing and great within my own sphere of influence. I'm not sure. What are you getting at?"

"Look, greatness is only relevant when you define it in a way that makes it most meaningful to YOU. Do you have kids?"

David nodded.

"Okay. As an example, if you can be a better dad, you've achieved at least one aspect of your own greatness. If being a good dad is something important to you, nobody can ever take that away from you. If it isn't something important to you, then you don't need to work on it."

David sat in thought. "So you are saying that greatness is whatever I desire?"

Regina smiled. "Not entirely. Mostly. Greatness, at least the way we talk about it, is elevating yourself. Becoming more you. Becoming a better you. If you aren't like Gandhi, but you think you should be, then you may not consider yourself great. It may even lead you to lower self-esteem and depression. But if you recognize that you aren't Gandhi, and will never be Gandhi, you can recognize that your own greatness will be different.

"Each of us has our own definition of greatness. Whether we admit it to ourselves or not, we all have an idea of what our own greatness looks like. Everyone has their own mission in life, their own way to improve the world around them. That's the greatness I'm talking about here. Living your best life."

David nodded slowly. "So you're not saying greatness is something achieved by only a few. Nor is it something only available to famous people. You're saying that greatness is far more personal, that it's different for everyone. That we need to define greatness for ourselves for it to be truly meaningful."

Regina smiled at David. "Exactly. The 5 Keys is an easy-to-remember framework designed to help you discover your own greatness.

"If we want to elevate our lives, how do we get started? What do we work on? What parts of our lives do we improve to change our lives for the better?

That's what the 5 Keys To Greatness are all about. To help each person improve their life, to find a new internal guiding light."

David nodded, as the purpose and the reasoning behind the 5 Keys To Greatness gained clarity. "So what are the 5 Keys To Greatness?"

Regina laughed again. "You cut right to the chase, huh?" She took a sip of her drink. "It is and it isn't that simple. I have people who explain the keys better than I do. My keyholders."

David nodded. "Pinch mentioned the keyholders."

Regina smirked. "And I thought I came up with that one. No matter." She shook her head, jokingly.

"Think of this as a little quest. A quest for you to rediscover sanity, to find the secrets to a good life."

David grinned. "You can't even give me a hint?"

Regina laughed. "I'll give you a hint. I'll also tell you what they are, briefly, so you don't keep wondering about it. The hint is that the 5 Keys spell out the word GREAT. Each key starts with one of the letters. This is helpful, because the framework gets deeper the more you contemplate it. You can remember it in a snap though, because you only have to remember the initials G.R.E.A.T."

"What does it stand for?"

Regina smiled. "Please promise me that you'll talk to my keyholders still."

David nodded, "Sure."

"Great." Regina and David both laughed at the pun.

"The keys are as follows:

"G is for Give, or to provide more to others.

"R is for Reason, or to have a purpose in life and at work.

"E is for Engage, or to be more present in the present moment.

"A is for Amazing, or to have a more positive attitude.

"T is for Tenacity, or to be more persistent.

"Not a single one of those will seem difficult. But each key can help you unlock your true destiny."

Regina gave him a half-grin. "Anything more than that will have to wait. You aren't the first person I've helped. My experience shows the most effective way to introduce the keys is by learning one key at a time. Each keyholder exemplifies one of the 5 Keys, making it valuable to learn directly from each of them."

David nodded. "Okay. That makes sense."

Regina sighed deeply, as though she finished a meal. She picked up her drink and leaned back, looking up at the dark night sky. David sat, waiting for her to continue. As she watched the sky, David realized she was finished. "So that's it?"

Regina laughed. "We'll go down in a minute and I'll give you Eddie's number. He's your first visit. Let's enjoy the stars for a few."

David started pulling his phone out of his pocket. Regina called, "No phones!" David slipped his phone back in his pocket, grabbed his beer, and leaned back as well. After a time Regina exhaled loudly and stood up. "Ready?"

"Yep." David stood. "Thanks for that little break. That was unexpected."

"Can you make it to Eddie tomorrow?"

David nodded. "That should be fine."

They grabbed their empty drinks, and walked down the narrow stairs. As they passed the doorway on the landing, David asked, "You live here?"

"Yeah. I love this place. Ever since I opened it, it has been a huge source of energy for me."

They reached the bottom of the stairs and the effusion of noise reached them. Regina hung her sweatshirt back up.

"It was great meeting you, David, and great talking to you." They walked to the bar. Regina went to the register, scribbled on a piece of paper. "Here is my number and Eddie's number. Give him a call tomorrow, meet up with him."

David took the slip of paper. "Thank you so much."

"Did you drive over?"

"Not tonight, going to grab a cab to get home."

Regina nodded as David said thank you once more

and left, hailing a cab. The bright yellow car swooped over. David climbed into the back seat.

"How are ya?!" The cab driver was exuberant.

"Hey." David was sitting in the backseat, reviewing everything he learned from Regina.

"How goes it?" Some cab drivers take their cue from their passengers; some want a conversation no matter what.

David nodded, still lost in thought. The cab driver glanced back at David, and merged onto the highway.

"What's wrong?" The driver asked David, turning around again. "Cat got your tongue?" The cabbie stared at him. David watched with concern as the cab veered out of its lane, and he pointed to the front. "Watch the road!"

The cabbie turned around, wrenched the wheel to the side to center the car. "Jeez, just tryin' to have a bit of a conversation. Don't be so lost inside yourself. You can tell me how you're doing, ya' know."

David sat back, on edge. His cab driver was not focused on the road.

"Things are going fine. I just finished a pretty deep conversation. Now I'm trying to get home to my family."

"Deep conversation, huh?" The cabbie turned back around to look at David. "Good old DMC, huh? Deep meaningful conversation?"

"Yes. Good old DMC." David sighed nervously, watching the passing cars edge closer. "Whoa! Watch out!"

The cab driver laughed, turned around, pulled the car back to the center of the lane. "What was it about?" He looked back at David.

David's eyes widened. "Stuff. Can you please watch the road?"

The cabbie laughed. "I've got it." He turned, then looked back at David. "I've been doing this for a long–"

BOOM. CRASH. EEEEERRRRRRRR. CRINCH!!

Neither the cabbie nor David noticed the red car shooting past in the next lane. The red car weaving in and out of traffic at high speeds and now passing them. Neither noticed the car taking too much space on the road. Neither noticed the red car using the outer edges of the lane, cutting closely in front of the other cars. As the red car flew past them, it tried to weave into their lane to get around a car. But it cut over too soon and slammed into the front fender of the cab.

The red car's back end spun out a little, then regained control. The driver sped away, fleeing the scene.

The cab started spinning, front end first. They flew into the next lane, slamming into the mangled guardrail. The force was too much, the damaged guardrail too low. The cab spun over the guardrail, landing on its roof on the embankment and then rolled over again, landing on the passenger side. The cab driver, belted in, sat stuck in his seat, hanging in the air, stunned. Some airbags deployed; the interior of the cab looked like a cloud.

David, unbelted in the back seat, lay against the door, on the ground, bloody, knocked about, hurting, hurting, hurting. Then the pain grew too much and he faded away.

03

The Hospital

DAVID HEARD A low steady beep, beep, beep in the distance. The sound drew nearer as events flooded back to him. All at once, David realized he was laying in a hospital bed, with machines beeping all around.

The room was dim. The walls were a muted beige, the furniture the drab green often seen in hospitals. David looked around, registered a man sitting in the chair by his bed.

"Oh thank goodness you're awake!" The chatty cabbie sat, twisting his cap around in his hands. "I didn't know what to think. That guy came out of nowhere, huh?"

David struggled to sit up as the pain washed over him. He felt bandages in different places, notably on his head. "My wife?"

The cabbie stood up. "I went through your pockets, I called the numbers I found. One guy, Eddie, had NO IDEA who you were. Ha! Isn't that funny?"

David stared at the man, expressionless.

The cabbie continued ignoring cues from David. "The other number, for a Regina or sometin', answered and she's on her way. The ambulance brought you here straight from the accident." The cabbie sat down, deflated. He sighed. "I needed that job. I can't believe that other guy did that." He shook his head.

David's patience wore thin. "Where's my phone?"

The cabbie brightened. "Oh, I got it right here." He started patting his pockets, looking for the phone. "Here it is." He handed it to David.

The nurse walked into the room. She was blonde, wearing blue scrubs, with her hair pulled back. "Hi there! Glad to see you woke up." She asked questions, to make sure he was okay. She asked his name, birthday, the date, and more. David went through the exercise, showing no apparent memory loss.

After she finished and started out of the room, David asked. "What's the damage?"

The nurse walked to his bed and grabbed his chart. "Well!"

"Hang on, please." David looked at the cabbie. "Look, I appreciate you coming out here with me, I do."

The cabbie, still twisting his cap, gave David a half-smile. "Okay. Okay. I get it. No problem-o, buddy. No problem." He stood up, held up an index card. "I wrote my number down on this card, with my insurance info. I also gave my information to the police, for the police report, so it should be in there as well."

He sighed, pulled his cap onto his head. He rubbed the back of his neck, worrying at it, and said, "Look, I'm sorry this happened. I couldn't control that bastard driving like that, the guy was probably a drunk. The cops want you to make a statement, so be expecting their call. And that lady Regina, she said she would come over—"

"I'm right here." Regina said, walking into the room.

"Oh, there she is. Okay. I'm really sorry, I don't think I did anything wrong, but I feel terrible. Call me if you need anything." He sighed loudly. The cabbie reached down to David's clothing, in a pile behind David, and shoved his card into a pocket. He walked out.

The nurse looked at Regina, then at David.

"Regina, can you give me a minute with the nurse?

We were about to go over some stuff."

Regina smiled and walked back out of the room.

"Okay, what's the damage?" David asked.

The nurse walked over to the side of the bed, looking through the chart. "You have a few minor cuts in different areas. Your arms, and a couple more on your head. The ones on your head the doctor stitched up. That's where most of the blood came from.

"The good news is, it doesn't look like you lost too much blood, just enough to make things look super scary." She continued down the list. "Some bruising on your legs, shoulders and ribs, which will look scary but go away. The ribs will make it painful to breath, talk, and more."

David chuckled, holding his chest as he did so. "Noticed that one already."

The nurse smiled, looking at David. "Taking over the counter pain relievers will help with that." She looked back at the chart. "Let's see. That's about it. No bones seem broken, but if you're feeling pain in a particular area, we can examine it more closely. As you move your limbs around, if there is any bad pain, numbness, or tingling, please let me know. The doctor will want to know." The nurse smiled at him. "The only other thing is the test results."

"Test results?"

She grimaced. "Yes. You hit your head pretty hard,

so we did a CT scan as a matter of course. While it looked fine, there were parts of it that concerned the doctor, so she asked for an MRI too." She sighed. "We're still waiting on the results."

David looked at her. "What did it find?"

"I don't know. They're waiting to interpret the images in more detail. And they will probably want to keep you overnight for observation."

David nodded as she put the chart back at the foot of his bed.

"I'll send your wife in."

David laughed. "She's not my wife."

The nurse gave him a look.

"Oh, not like that. She's like a teacher, a life coach. That cabbie, he called random numbers he found in my pocket, and she was one of them."

The nurse laughed, shaking her head. She walked around the room then, checked the machines, straightened up, then walked out.

Regina walked in, slowly. "How are you?"

David grimaced. "Not great. Not terrible, but not great."

Regina nodded. "Did anybody call your wife? Your family?"

David shook his head. "I was about to." He held up the cell phone.

Regina nodded. "Go ahead."

David picked up the phone, dialed, held the phone to his ear. He waited, then spoke softly. His emotion was apparent. They spoke a little longer. Finally he expressed his love, and put the phone down.

"She's trying to find a babysitter, to come see me. I told her at least you're here."

Regina smiled, sat down.

"Well David, that is a first. The first time that what I said to someone was so impactful, they tried to end it all."

David laughed. "Real nice of you." He grimaced from the pain in his ribs. "Ow! These bruises don't make laughter easy." He sighed. "I don't know how it happened. The cabbie was strange, trying to talk to me all the time, not paying attention to the road. An accident was likely, I think. But what happened was probably unavoidable."

"How so?"

"This red car, it came flying out of nowhere, clipped us in the front and we spun out. Crazy how a life can be flipped upside down in only an instant."

The machines continued to beep. The nurse bustled back in with a dark-haired lady, wearing horn-rimmed glasses. The new lady was pretty in an everyday way, wearing a white coat. "Here's Dr. Monaghan."

The doctor walked over to David and introduced herself with a big smile. "Hi, how are you? Well, aside from the obvious!" They laughed. "I'm the neurologist on call."

David looked at her. "Neurologist?"

She laughed. "Yes. You banged your head up pretty good there. When there was an abnormality on the CT scan, we sent you for an MRI. I want to talk to you about that." She looked at Regina. "Should I discuss it now, or . . ." She trailed off, looking at Regina.

Regina smiled and stood up. "Don't worry. I'll wait outside. I know, HIPAA and all that."

David waved her off. "Sit down. It's fine. I would rather someone be here for this."

Regina's smile disappeared, and she sat down.

Dr. Monaghan said, "Okay, first the good news. The CT scan and the MRI both showed no major damage from the car accident. If you push us, we can let you go tonight. I would rather not do that, to be safe. It would be best if you stay the night, but based on all available data, you may not have to."

David nodded. "Fair enough. And the bad news?"

Dr. Monaghan sighed. "It always comes to that." She laughed, with a little bitterness in her voice. "The first thing I will point out is that everything is inconclusive. We need to do more tests, when the bruising and swelling go down."

David narrowed his eyes, looked at her. "What is it?"

Dr. Monaghan sighed again. "I'm not sure. It could be nothing. We saw some abnormalities in the CT scan, and then in the MRI. Whatever it is, it could be nothing, brought on by the accident. It could also be a benign abnormality. We'll know more once the swelling is down."

David sharply breathed in. He forced the air out loudly. "But what is it?"

Dr. Monaghan looked at him briefly, then dropped her eyes. "I don't want to alarm you. But there's a chance it could be a tumor. Maybe there is a twenty to thirty percent chance that what we saw is a tumor. There are one or two other possibilities; but those are very, very unlikely. Figure half a percent chance or so."

Regina reached over and took David's hand. Her face looked pained. David took the proffered hand, held it tightly, watched the doctor. "What about the other one or two things it could be?"

Dr. Monaghan smiled a little. "If you demand it, I have to tell you. But they are so unlikely, I would rather not bring it up until I have to. Potentially long-term debilitating illnesses. Should I elaborate?"

David's breathing was fast. His spinning head spun faster, spun more, he felt the world reeling around him. He looked around for support, for help from the onslaught of feelings.

Regina looked at David, saw that he was not coping

well. She looked at Dr. Monaghan. "Can he make that decision later?"

"Definitely." She smiled, looking at David. "In fact, I encourage it." She took a deep breath, shifted around the bed a little, put the chart back in the bed.

"Look, David. The news isn't bad. Not yet. The news is mostly good. Think of it as a hurricane out at sea, with only a twenty-five percent chance of making landfall. But if it makes landfall, it lands on your doorstep."

David tried to calm down as Dr. Monaghan continued. "Even if it makes landfall, it could be minor. And even if it is a major issue, it may not cause that much damage." She paused. "I wanted you to know what is going on. I wanted to make sure that you know what we saw. But I don't want to alarm you. There is no need for worry. Not yet. We will tackle whatever this is, one step at a time. There is so much that can still happen, so much that we don't know. The best thing you can do for now is remain calm."

David nodded slightly, still holding Regina's hand. The tension, the emotion in the room, was thick, palpable, ready to break by the slightest change.

A light knock sounded at the door. A lady peeked her head in, saw David, breathed a sigh of relief. She walked in, saw Regina, saw her holding hands with David, and frowned.

"Who's this?"

"Hey, you made it." David smiled at her. "Serena, this is Regina, the bartender that guy sent me to, for the 5 Keys To Greatness. She came when the cabdriver called her. Regina, meet my wife, Serena." He realized he was still holding Regina's hand, and let it go. "And this is Dr. Monaghan. She's a neurologist here. She was telling me what they saw in my brain." He laughed ruefully, held up his hand. "That's actually when Regina grabbed my hand. While Dr. Monaghan was dropping a potential bomb."

Regina stood up. "I'll wait outside for a bit," she said, "I have to get going soon anyway."

Dr. Monaghan smiled, looked at both David and Serena. "I'll give you two a few. I'm around if you need me, let me know if you have more questions."

They left the room, leaving David and Serena alone. Serena looked at David, her bright blue eyes wide and concerned. She sat down, and David brought her up to speed. He told her about his night, visiting Regina, their rooftop conversation, the wild cab ride. He told her about waking up in the hospital, about the cab driver calling numbers in his pocket until he found someone. "Calling random numbers in some random guy's pocket." Serena laughed.

Serena learned about the moment right before she walked in. About how there might be bad news . . . or not.

Serena gave David a hard look. The room was quiet, save for the incessant beep of the machines. She took a deep breath, then said, "Okay. I wasn't ready for that."

David laughed mirthlessly. "Neither was I. Kind of an eye opener, huh?"

Dr. Monaghan knocked at the door. "Hi guys. I wanted to check on you before I finish my rounds." Dr. Monaghan walked in so she could see both David and Serena. Dr. Monaghan looked at David. "May I speak candidly in front of your wife?"

David nodded.

"As I told you before, I can answer any questions you have, but I'd rather wait until we know more. There is nothing we can do right now to improve anything, no matter what. Try not to worry about this–or to worry as little as possible," she smiled. "I know sometimes worry is impossible to escape, but do your best to remain hopeful."

Dr. Monaghan continued, "That car accident may be really good for you. If there is a major issue, or even a minor issue, the earlier it is found, the better the prognosis."

Dr. Monaghan gave them a grim smile, and asked if there were more questions. She made David promise he would follow up at her office, and asked about staying the night. "I can't force you, but I do recommend it."

David and Serena discussed it quickly, then agreed

he would stay.

"The babysitter only had about an hour, dear, so I have to get back. This hospital is so far away. We'll come pick you up in the morning." Serena leaned over and kissed David, her eyes glistening with tears unspilled.

As she pulled away, David grabbed her arm. "Hey. Hey, look at me."

She looked at him, tears brimming in her eyes. Dr. Monaghan looked away.

"Don't worry, we'll make it through this. Okay? Promise me you won't worry."

Serena looked away. Tears rolled down her face, quietly blazing wet trails along her cheeks, as she fell apart. David reached out his arms and enveloped her while she sobbed silently.

Dr. Monaghan looked over Serena's shoulder at David and waved; David gave her a slight wave as she turned and left.

Serena slowly calmed down. She sat up. "I have to send the babysitter home."

David nodded, and then said, "I'll see you in the morning. Don't worry."

Serena nodded.

David looked at her and said, "Remember what Mark Twain said about worry." He smiled. "'I've lived through some terrible things in my life, some of which actually happened.' We need to focus on what-is, not on what-ifs. The kids need it. We need it."

Serena nodded again. She left, walking slowly, breathing deeply, the gravity of the situation still fresh in her mind.

04

Living Your Best Life

REGINA WALKED BACK into the room. "Serena told me she has to leave. I also have to get going, but I can sit with you a bit longer if you want."

David looked at her. "Thank you. I'd appreciate that." He gestured to the chair by the bed. "This is a lot to take in."

Regina sat down, and a silence settled around them. The events of the night were so intense that the silence felt relaxed and empty.

"It's funny, you know," David began, "the whole

reason I met Pinch."

Regina straightened, a funny look on her face as David mentioned Pinch. "What do you mean?"

"Well, I went to these cliffs I used to go to when I was younger. They sit above the highway, you have to hike a little to get to them. We used to call them the 'Cliffs of Despair,' a play on that movie The Princess Bride. I was having a really hard day, a really hard time. I was under a lot of stress and I went to those cliffs. I don't know what would have happened. Most likely I would have sat up there, blown off steam for a while and then gone home. Probably that would be it. But when I climbed up there, I was definitely not okay. Like, not okay." David looked at Regina, to see absolution, to see understanding.

Regina nodded slowly. "I've been to some pretty dark places in my life. I think I told you that before. Go on."

"I was up there for only a few minutes, getting it all together, when Pinch showed up. It's hard to believe it was only yesterday. I tried every normal, polite way to tell him that I didn't want him there. Body language, words, attitude, everything, short of telling him to go away." David laughed. "He ignored it all."

"What happened?"

"He sat down next to me, asked if I needed anything. He listened a little, sat with me a lot, and eventually sent me to come see you. And here I am." David shrugged.

"There I was, at the top of those cliffs, and I didn't care. If I had fallen down accidentally, in that moment, I couldn't care less. I didn't care anymore!!" David smoothed out the sheet laying over his body.

"Now here I am, sitting in the hospital, finding out I really may be dying." Regina tried to interrupt, but he motioned for her to stay quiet. "I know, I know, it's only a chance, but I'm making a point. So here I am, and I really may be dying. And the only feeling I have inside is this deep, deep desire to live, to live at all costs, to achieve things with my life. To DO." David held his arms out wide, then grimaced from the pain in his ribs. He put his arms down and sighed.

Regina nodded. "Sometimes what we have is valued the most when it is most fragile, when it is most threatened. Before, maybe you were too caught up in the moment to recognize what you had. Now that it's threatened, you can see so much more, and you have clarity on all the good things that you have. That clarity gives you the strength to fight back, to seize the day."

David nodded. "That makes sense."

Regina went on. "Look. This is a big part of the 5 Keys To Greatness, helping people live their best lives. I know we covered this. But people throughout the world don't feel connected. They can't plug in to their own lives, to their own circumstances, in order to move forward and excel. That's what the 5 Keys To Greatness are all about.

"We can activate tremendous powers within our own lives if we open up to the experience. We can apply the right tools, the right mindset and unlock our own greatness. Unlocking enables us to help those around us more fully."

Regina sighed. "You should know that it takes constant effort. You work on it, better at some times, worse at others. For instance, sometimes I'm great at keeping a journal, and other times, I can't find the time. Even though I know it helps a lot."

"How long have you been on this journey?" David asked.

Regina looked at her hands, did some quick math. "Oh, about 5 years. That is around the same time that I bought the restaurant and started climbing out of my own little 'pit of despair.'" They laughed at Regina's additional reference to The Princess Bride.

"What's the most relevant part of the 5 Keys To Greatness?" David asked.

Regina looked at David, glanced at the clock, looked back at David. "Before I answer, what would you say is the most important aspect of living your best life? Of living a life of purpose?"

David shrugged. "I don't know. Maybe being more aware of the things around you. Maybe being more driven. Maybe having more clarity about your purpose in life. Maybe connecting more with the people around you." He looked up at the ceiling. "Trying to be positive about things in life can certainly make a difference. But what's to stop someone from getting discouraged with how difficult it all is? To just give up?"

Regina grinned as she listened to David. "David, you're right about all of those. I think you'll really connect well to the 5 Keys To Greatness.

"Each of the keys helps someone be more in tune with his or her own life. Each key leads someone to living his or her best life in a special way.

"Living your best life means being all you can be at anything you do. The United States Army used to say to 'be all you can be.' Not to be a superman. To live true to your own potential. To be all that you can be.

"If you observe people, you'll see that every person you meet has a different skill set. Different things they are good at, different things they like to do, different things they hate to do. Different strengths, different weaknesses, we are all so different. If you observe even just physical characteristics, everyone is different. Different hair, different eyes, different builds, different struggles.

"People are entirely different. They say if you compare all the fingerprints out there, you will never find two that match. Both now and in the past. Seven and a half billion people and there is not a single fingerprint match. Include all those who lived before us and the number is staggering.

"But this is the point. Be the best part of you. Live your own best life. Recognize that we all have things we are good at, things we are not good at, and everything in between.

"Now add in the 5 Keys To Greatness. It's an easy-to-remember toolset to help you unlock your destiny, to help you find the greatness within you. It's simple on purpose so anyone can remember it. Just remember the word GREAT and what each letter means. As you contemplate each key, you will find more depth, more sub-categories. Then you continue to perfect it, applying it to your life, and you'll discover even more ways to implement that key.

"There are systems out there meant to be motivational. They get so complex it's hard to put them into practice. You need notes, notebooks, and guides, you need step-by-step instructions, and much more. The 5 Keys To Greatness is set up to make it easy to remember, easy to use. Simple yet complex. Shallow to grasp, yet you can go as deep as you want.

"One of my biggest desires is to see as many people

as possible activate themselves. I want to see these keys impact people all around the world. Together, we can build a world of people living their best lives–living true and fulfilling their purpose.

"The saddest thing is a person wasting their life, while the most amazing thing is a person on their way to greatness. I've seen this. I've seen people come in to Vantage Point who look like they have nothing. I've also seen people come in who knew exactly what they were about." Regina took a deep breath, blew it out slowly. "It changes someone completely."

David stared at her, nodding. A moment passed. He processed her words, felt out her statements, the impassioned pleas.

Regina changed the subject, saying seriously, "But you are one lucky fellow."

"What, the accident?"

She smiled. "Maybe. I was talking about Pinch. Nobody has seen him in years. We thought he died, truthfully. I guess he's still out there, spreading his ideas, though he makes me do the hard work." She laughed. "Most of the people who come to me heard of the 5 Keys To Greatness from people they know. Pinch hasn't sent me anyone in a long time. You must be one special guy, for Pinch to hike up there for you."

"What do you mean?"

Regina shook her head slowly. "Nothing in

particular; he was getting older the last time I saw him. Hiking can't be easy for him.

"Look, this is part of our current culture. Everyone is incredibly special. Remember that. We are all different, with our own goals and dreams. But culturally, we forget how special we are. Or we're encouraged to forget it, I don't know."

Regina looked at David a little closer. "But you? I think there is something extra special about you. I can't quite place my finger on it. I'll bet Pinch could tell us, if he were here.

"Remember, sometimes those of us who hit the darkest places are the same ones who shine the brightest light."

David paraphrased this to himself. "Those who find the darkest darkness also shine the brightest light."

"You should feel honored that Pinch himself told you to come to me. He created this framework. He taught it to many of us, and now we pay it forward by teaching it to others."

"But he told me that someone else taught him!"

Regina laughed. "Back when he was around, he said that all the time. He's deflecting the credit, that's all. I'm almost positive he created it himself, to bring more light into the world."

Regina looked at the clock again. "Oof. It's late. I have to get going." Regina grabbed her bag, stood up.

"You'll see Eddie tomorrow, then come by the bar?"

"I'll try to."

Regina smiled. "David, I mean this in the nicest way possible. You narrowly escaped death. You don't know what's on the other side of those brain scans. Hug and kiss your kids, then go see Eddie. Let's treat the 5 Keys To Greatness like it is the most important thing in your life right now. No matter how much time you have left, it will make a huge impact on every second."

David nodded. "Okay. Tomorrow."

Regina waved and left.

05

The 1ˢᵗ Key: Give / Provide

D AVID WALKED UP to the the investment firm's building. He admired the large building, with marble flowing straight up, and large windows, bright and inviting. The modern lines of the building felt inspiring and invoked a sense of excitement in David.

David walked in, noticing the line of barricades and security. Instead of turnstiles, they had clear plexiglass barriers that whooshed in and out as people scanned their key cards to enter and exit.

David went to the security kiosk. "Hi, I'm here to

see Eddie Roth."

The guard looked at David, scanning him. He gave David a huge smile. "Eddie? Eddie's great. Hang on, let me check. I'll need your ID."

David handed his ID over while the guard typed on his computer. He scanned the license, then printed a temporary badge.

"Here you go! Use the south elevators. Eighteenth floor, ask reception and he'll show you where. And tell Eddie that Jack says hi!"

David was perplexed at the guard's familiarity with Eddie. He went to the elevators, passing by the fountain, catching a whiff of the chlorine in the water. He noted the muted plants, the interior slabs of marble mixed with textured glass, finished off with a quiet gold-colored metal.

David went to the eighteenth floor and told the man at reception he was here to see Eddie.

"Welcome! So glad to have you. Right this way."

David walked through the pristine hallways with him, along the tan carpet. They passed many glass-walled offices filled with sharp espresso furniture with chrome-colored accents.

David was shown to a conference room, which continued the espresso and chrome color theme. Everything except the conference table. The conference table was a slab of granite, with a stunning river of color and motion flowing through the middle. As David looked closer, he realized the table was two pieces of granite, matched well in the middle.

"Eddie will be right out. Have a seat if you like." The receptionist gave David a huge smile, waved at the table and chairs, and left.

David walked around the room, admiring the craftsmanship of the conference table. Before long, the glass door opened.

"Hey! Are you David? I'm Eddie."

David smiled and walked over, hand extended. They shook hands.

Eddie asked, "What happened to your head?" He pointed to David's bandages, smaller but still there.

David explained about the car accident, the hospital. "Oh, that was that random call last night?" Eddie asked, as David nodded. Eddie asked David how he was doing. David told him that overall he was fine.

"Can I get you a coffee? Or a water?"

"Coffee please."

"All right, come on then." Eddie beckoned David to follow him. "So, you're going through the 5 Keys To Greatness?"

David said, "Yes, I am."

"And got started from no less than Pinch, huh?" Eddie continued walking, leading David into a kitchen area.

David laughed. "Yes. Still trying to figure that one out."

Eddie walked up to a large, fancy-looking espresso machine. Eddie started playing with buttons, levers, and knobs, then stopped and looked at David.

"Do you prefer light, medium, or dark roast?"

"Light, please. You have all those?"

Eddie laughed. "I gave you the cliff notes version. We actually have a decent selection of coffee from all over the world in every roast. Do you prefer espresso or coffee? Pretend you're at a fancy coffee shop; how would you order?"

David laughed. "Wow. Okay, how about a latte, about medium sized? No sugar."

Eddie reached over, grabbed coffee beans, put them through a grinder. He made the latte, complete with frothed milk. After handing the plain white cup to David, Eddie showed him where the fixings were. Eddie then made himself a coffee.

"Come on, let's sit down."

Eddie led the way to a corner seating area, complete with couches, tables and chairs. A few people sat enjoying a snack or a coffee. The floor ran right into the window, where the view stretched out in front of them. The tall windows gave a view of the city unlike anything David had seen. Eddie pointed out an area, and they sat down, in two overstuffed chairs with a table between.

"How much did Regina tell you?"

"She told me to remember the word GREAT as a tool to remember the keys. And what each key is. Not much more than that. At the hospital, we also discussed living your best life."

"Okay. As a refresher, the words to remember are Give, Reason, Engage, Amazing, and Tenacity. G–R–E–A–T. Today we're going to talk about giving, or to provide. As Audrey Hepburn was known for saying, 'Giving is living.'

David nodded. Eddie went on. "Give. Provide. Have you ever done something for someone else, something incredible?"

David thought back to when he chased after an old man who dropped his wallet. David missed the light and watched him get into a cab, only to follow the man in a second cab to return the wallet. He nodded. "Yes, I've done something like that."

"How did you feel? Not only while you were doing it, but afterward, the rest of the day, the rest of the week, for as long as it was fresh in your mind?"

David thought about how he felt that day, and the days after. "I felt really good. In fact, that amazing feeling carried with me for a long time." David took a deep breath. "Even you bringing it up now, brings that pleasure and pride back to light."

"Yes! That's it! That feeling, it lifts you to cloud

nine and keeps you there. Sometimes for days. You see, giving is not really you losing out. When you give, someone else gains, but you gain as well. All by giving your time, your money, your thoughts, your resources! Giving unlocks tremendous benefits for you! It's almost a contradiction. It seems as if you should be worse off after giving, but in truth you are almost always better off.

"Do you remember Anne Frank? She's that girl who kept a diary while hiding from the Nazis with her family. She kept a diary while they were locked away, hiding, in two small rooms above her father's factory. They lived there for years with family and friends. The Nazis killed her in the concentration camps before the war ended, but her father found her diary after the war and published it. She wrote, 'No one has ever become poor by giving.'" Eddie took a sip of coffee. "Do you hear that? 'No one has ever become poor by giving.' She wrote with a wisdom that belied her age.

"The more you integrate giving into your life, the more you'll see how wonderful it is. You'll benefit in unexpected ways, and so will everyone around you. As you give more and more, people in turn give more to those around them, and the whole world benefits.

"Now, you can give things like money and food to people. This is definitely important. You should always give charity, when and where possible. You do need to keep it under control though–don't give everything away, that doesn't make sense. Why should you need to accept gifts from others because you gave too much? But a person should give a small percentage, say five or ten percent, of their income. This is a good tithe when income is sufficient.

"You can also give intangibles like advice, friendship, attention, forgiveness, and respect. You can gift whatever you want to people. The more you call it like it is–a gift, something you gave–the more you can pat yourself on the back for having done so."

David put his coffee down. "How do you give forgiveness? And isn't it wrong to pat yourself on the back?"

Eddie leaned forward. "I'm glad you asked! Nope!" He laughed. "Well, I should clarify. Let's cover one at a time. If you forgive someone even if every part of you says no, you have given forgiveness.

"Don't let people walk all over you. This is not healthy. There will be times that you need to stand up for yourself. If you are making a conscious decision to forgive, it is your choice. You can give people a gift of forgiveness whenever you want.

"The same goes for other intangibles. Let's say you don't have the time or the brain space to listen to someone's problems and give advice. You can make a conscious effort to slow down and listen to them long enough to give advice.

"Does giving intangibles make sense now?"

David nodded, absorbing Eddie words.

"Great." Eddie smiled. "You asked if it's wrong to pat yourself on the back. Others may feel differently, but I say no. You have to recognize the good you have done. You have to recognize the difference you made in the lives of those around you. It helps with your self-esteem and more.

"Keep in mind, I'm only talking about being honest with yourself–not gloating. If someone uses things they do to be arrogant, or to lie to themselves, I don't think that is healthy or wise."

Eddie picked up his coffee and sat back. He breathed deeply, looking out the expansive windows for a minute, then he turned back to David.

"I could go on about this all day. About this feeling of floating on clouds that comes with giving. About how the more you give, the more you get. Winston Churchill, the oft-quoted British Prime Minister, said 'We make a living by what we get, but we make a life by what we give.' Giving lifts you up, infuses you with your own self-worth. It's one of the best ways to build yourself back up when you are feeling down. Just give!! Find ways to give and then do it.

"And you can give anything. Big or small, quick or time-consuming, to people you know, or to people you don't know, it doesn't matter. It has a positive effect on you either way."

Eddie jumped up. "Come on, I want to show you something. We can talk on the way."

David stood and asked, "Where are we going?"

"You'll see. Unless you're really short on time." David shook his head as Eddie led the way to the elevators.

Eddie slowed by each person he saw to greet them warmly, ask about their day, their family, their life.

David saw how Eddie gave each person his full attention as they moved along.

In the elevator, Eddie turned to David. "Did you see that?"

"Yes, you were giving them time and attention, right?"

Eddie smiled, "Yes! And I wasn't doing it selfishly, by the way. I love giving, and that was the way I could do so most effectively at the moment.

"We have many opportunities to give on a daily basis. But I see people all the time who don't give because they think they need to do a grand gesture. Simple is the answer!

"What's one of the most precious gifts of all? Imagine a four-year-old boy who wants to give his mother something. So he looks around, sees a dandelion in the lawn–this bright, beautiful, stunning yellow flower. He picks it. He holds it tightly in his small hand so as not to lose it, and gives it to his mother. This limp weed, this flower, with a mangled stem, is one of the truest expressions of love and giving in the world.

"If you ever get worried that a gift is not enough, think of little kids and flowers. Think of the dandelion, the red clover, the little buttercup. It's these simple gifts that show the recipient, 'I love you,' or 'I care.' It shows it in the simplest way. Grand gestures often can't compete with simplicity."

The elevator dinged. David followed Eddie through the lobby, past the security guard from earlier. Eddie greeted him warmly, asked him, "How'd your girlfriend like those tickets, my man?"

The guard beamed. "She loved them. They made her day. Eddie, you're the man. Thank you!" The guard's eyes sparkled with excitement.

Eddie smiled. "It was my absolute pleasure."

They continued into the garage, toward a brand new, sleek, four-door Tesla.

Eddie looked at David. "I gave him tickets that I couldn't use anyway. When I can't use my tickets, I try to spread the wealth to many people. But it's the first time I could help him out. Here I am, some guy from the 18th floor, handing over very good tickets to him. How do you think that makes him feel?"

David saw that the question wasn't rhetorical. "Good?"

"Yes, but so much more than that, it makes him feel important. Imagine, he tells his girlfriend that a big shot from the 18th floor, a guy he's friendly with, gave him tickets. For free. Because of her. Now he feels important, and he makes her feel important. My small gift has turned into a new gift, that he has spread to others."

They got into the car. David noticed the stunning wood trim, the luxurious leather seats, and the carefully designed interior. "It's also important to give to yourself when you can. I spend a lot of time in the car, and I can more than afford it. No one has to know how nice the interior is. The base model of this car is quite affordable. Personally, I dislike it when I see people driving cars they can't afford because they think they deserve it."

Eddie turned the car on, as David buckled in. "Albert Einstein actually talked about this. He said 'The value of a man resides in what he gives, and not in what he is capable of receiving.' There are aspects to our self-worth that are tied to our ability to give to others."

Eddie drove, while he continued. "Can you think of a season of giving? For Christians, it is Christmas time, when everyone talks about 'Christmas spirit.' For Jews, it's the high holidays, when everyone is busy giving charity and feeling charitable toward others. The first key is about bringing some of this giving spirit into the rest of the year.

"Look, there will always be people who need you, your time or your money. Some of these people may be related to you, some not. Some you may know, some you may have never met before. Open your eyes so you can see these needs around you, and then give."

Eddie pulled his wallet out as they pulled up to a bank's ATM. He punched buttons on the machine, taking out cash.

He grabbed the stack of twenties and drove on. "Here." Eddie handed the wad of cash to David.

This snapped David out of his reverie. "Huh?! What are you doing?"

"Just hold on to it for a little. I don't do this with everyone, but let's go have some fun."

"What do you mean?"

"Thank the Lord, I'm wealthy enough. Giving away a few hundred dollars doesn't affect my finances, but it is awesome to do. Let's go around and give it out. We can do anything. We can go to a grocery store and pay someone's bill. We can go to a drive-through to pay for the person behind us, which often results in a giving chain. We can give the money to people on the street. We can do whatever you want! What do you think?

Which do you want to do?"

David thought back to times when groceries for his family were hard to get. "Let's go to a grocery store. Is there one nearby?"

"I have one in mind. Let's go."

Eddie continued, "Giving is good to implement in all aspects of your life. That's why it's one of the 5 Keys To Greatness. But sometimes it can be hard to fully integrate giving.

"I have a quick exercise you can use for giving. It shouldn't take long. If you spend too much time doing it, you won't want to do it the next time.

"Your goal should be to do this at least once a day. At any moment you can look around to identify one small thing you can give to someone else. It should be small, manageable, and quick to do.

"If you do it at work, it can be as simple as smiling at a co-worker. Yes, this counts! By the way, giving a smile is fantastic in that it spreads like wildfire." Eddie grinned, looked at David, who smiled back, proving his point.

"As soon as you identify what to do, do it! No procrastinating, no second-guessing, nothing. If you are at home and you think about doing the dishes–don't delay! Do it right away." Eddie chuckled as he pulled into a parking spot.

They walked into a grocery store which was shabby

around the edges. Eddie said, "It's best to do this when you're already in line. Let's grab a drink or something."

They chose drinks from a fridge. The store wasn't busy. Only a few people were checking out.

"There," Eddie whispered, pointing to a lady struggling with a young child, bringing her cart to the register. She was wearing lightly faded clothing, so lightly that it was barely noticeable. Her little boy kept trying to climb out of the cart while she unloaded her groceries. Frustrated, she picked up her son and put him on the ground.

David and Eddie stood behind her. She unloaded her groceries onto the belt and juggled the roving child. She noticed them, with only drinks to buy. "Do you want to go ahead?"

Eddie smiled, shook his head. "No thanks."

They watched in silence as she watched the bill grow larger. Beep. Beep. She moved her cart to the end of the checkout, where the bagger placed her groceries into the cart. The lady stood near the payment terminal nervously, holding the small boy.

David and Eddie watched her. David's heart was going a million miles a minute, getting more and more nervous.

The last item went over the scanner. The man working the checkout told her the total. It was over two hundred dollars. The lady slowly pulled her debit card from her purse.

Eddie pushed David. David walked over. "I've got it."

The lady and the man both ignored him. Her card was almost in the payment terminal when David reached over, pushing her hand down. "I've got it."

Now she looked at him. She didn't understand what was happening.

"Umm, ah, I–" David pulled the cash out of his pocket, showed it to the clerk, motioned to the drinks, and said, "Please add these groceries to my bill. Scan the drinks. I'll pay for it all."

The clerk was stunned. "You can't do that."

Eddie looked at the clerk. "Why not?"

The clerk stared at them. "I–I don't know."

The lady started tearing. "Ah–are you sure?"

David and Eddie smiled at her. David said, "Yes. Absolutely. Go take care of your son. Have a fantastic day. Enjoy yourself."

The clerk rolled his eyes, and said, "Whatever." He grabbed the drinks, adding them to the bill, and told David, "That will be two forty three twenty."

David counted off thirteen twenties and handed it to the cashier. The lady, seeing that David was serious, whispered, "Thank you." And then, still tearing at the eyes, she repeated, "Thank you. That means so much right now."

David and Eddie gave her a small wave, as she put

her son back into the cart and rolled out of the store.

After getting change, David and Eddie walked out of the store. "So? How did it feel?"

David relived the rush. He closed his eyes and breathed deeply. "That . . .felt . . . amazing!" David held his arms up and out, filling his body with air and exhilaration.

Eddie laughed. "Come on, let's go give the rest away."

They walked down the street to a restaurant. Eddie asked David for a twenty before they walked in. Eddie asked the hostess for a table with a server who needed a big tip as he palmed her the twenty.

She brought them to a corner of the restaurant. A few minutes later a young man came over to take their order. They each ordered something small. While they waited for the food to come out, Eddie continued. "Many people feel lost and hopeless. It's part of the normal human condition. Not to stay like that, that's not good. Hope brings so much into a person's life. But it's normal to feel like that periodically.

"When we give to others, whatever we give, it opens us up and helps us get past those feelings. Think about how you felt with that lady before. Do you feel bigger, better now?"

David looked at Eddie, eyes shining. "Yes, it felt really good. I remember times when someone doing that to my grocery bill would have made a huge difference."

"Exactly! She's having a hard time. We all go through hard times. Financial hardships, difficult relationships, whatever. But when we connect with the people around us, when we see that we're not in it alone, everything is easier. Giving to others makes this connection more obvious."

The food arrived. Eddie asked for the check, and they started to snack. Eddie continued, "It's almost like a reconnection. Giving reconnects us with others, and to ourselves. Giving opens us up so it's easier to move past feeling lost and hopeless.

"Giving infuses us with a sense of purpose and belonging. Whether you're giving to people you love, or to perfect strangers, any giving you do helps you on your way to greatness.

"You can volunteer for organizations. You can hold the door open for someone. You can smile. You can do things that are effortless or things that are hard. No matter what, it improves you. It helps you spark the greatness within."

The check arrived. Eddie and David talked while finishing their snack. Eddie looked at David. "Do you want to leave the rest of the money? Or should we give a couple of twenties away to homeless people on the way back?"

David grinned. "Let's do that." He pulled out two twenties, putting everything else into the server book, leaving a tip of over one hundred dollars. He grabbed the pen, wrote 'thank you' in big letters, with a smiley face.

Eddie and David walked out of the restaurant, got back into the car. Eddie asked, "How did that feel?"

David laughed. "Wow. This is really fun! It's wonderful how a small act, which clearly benefits him, can bring me so much joy." He climbed into the car and pulled out the last two twenties. "Here."

Eddie took one, leaving the other in David's hand. "You do one, I'll do one. Come on." Eddie drove off.

As they drove, they saw someone with a gathering of belongings on the sidewalk. Pedestrians gave this person a wide berth. Eddie looked at David, as if to ask, him? David nodded. Eddie slowed and pulled the car up to the curb.

David got out and walked to the person. The person shied away from David a little. David knelt down, held out the money. "Here. For you."

The person slowly reached over, cautious, so cautious, hand out, extended . . . then snatched the bill. The person examined the bill carefully, ignoring David.

David stood up and went back to the car.

"Many of these people are suffering from more than just homelessness," said Eddie, as they pulled away from the curb. "I'm actually glad that happened. Don't ever take it personally if someone is unwilling or unable to acknowledge what you do. Some of the most influential giving is when it's impossible for the recipient to say thank you. Like that server in the restaurant. He can't say thank you unless we go back there. Does that diminish what we did?"

David thought about it. "Not at all."

"Exactly." They pulled up to a light. A man stood on the median, holding a sign saying he was a disabled veteran, asking for money. Eddie rolled down the window, held out the twenty.

"Oh, God bless! Oh, God bless!" The man cried, taking the bill. "Thank you!!"

The light turned green. Eddie turned the wheel to the left and started driving. "By the way, one important thing I don't think I mentioned. Giving is unique to you. The way you give won't be the same as the way I give. Or anyone else.

"As an example, I'm financially stable. I can do things like this without making a dent in my finances. But for someone without a lot of money, doing this is crazy.

"But you can do something like this with less money. It's a similar outcome. For instance, if you gave that lady $20, it still would have helped. Not quite the same, but it definitely works. If we tipped that server a twenty on that bill, it wouldn't be the same impact, but it's still a big tip, relatively. See what I'm saying?"

David nodded, thinking it all through.

"I have to get back to work now. Do you get the idea?"

David nodded. "Yes. Thank you."

Eddie's building appeared at the end of the street. "I'm checking in with Regina tonight, so I'll run over it all again with her."

"Fantastic," said Eddie. "Remember to make it your own. Think about how it makes the most sense for you, and then do it. That's the main idea." He pulled back into the garage and parked his car. They walked into the building together. David returned his security badge to the guard and thanked Eddie. Eddie smiled, shook his hand, and walked to the elevators.

* * *

David walked into Vantage Point to see Regina. It was afternoon so the place was mostly empty; people were eating at a few tables.

David walked up to the bar and sat down. Regina noticed him and came over.

David said, "I have to get home, but I wanted to connect with you first."

Regina smiled. "Great! This is important, to internalize concepts and to process what you learn. I recommend that you write up your thoughts and ideas on each key as you finish learning it. Call it journaling, a diary, notes, or whatever you want, as long as you do it. Writing is a great tool to help your brain remember things for the long term." Regina put her hands on the bar in front of her. "Want anything to drink?"

David nodded. "Water please."

Regina filled a glass and put it down in front of David. She put her hands together. "Want to tell me some of what you learned today?"

"Sure, I can review it quickly. Give is the first key, as you know. Or, as Eddie said, giving is living.

"Giving is a big part of discovering your own greatness. If someone is living a selfish life, he or she may feel lost and hopeless. Giving brings our focus to the broader world and helps get rid of these feelings.

"Giving helps to reconnect us to ourselves and those around us. Eddie said that giving infuses us with a sense of purpose and belonging."

"Among other things." Regina smiled. "Go on."

"You can give to anyone: strangers, family, whomever. You should also give to yourself by indulging in a little self-care. Giving can be big or small, including a smile or holding the door open for someone." David took a sip of water.

"Eddie also told me that giving is selfish." David saw Regina's face and laughed. "Or maybe self-serving. In that you usually get more than you give."

Regina waited to see if David would continue. Not that he needed to; he covered the most important points. And of course, each key needs to cater to the self. When she saw he was done, she mimicked a slow clap, with a smile to show her sincerity.

"Well done. Bravo." Regina grinned. "This is great. You're moving right along."

She walked to the register and rummaged around. "Hang on, I've got it here somewhere," she mumbled, as she continued looking. "Ah! Here it is!"

Regina walked back over with a slip of paper. "Tomorrow you visit Ezra. Can you write this down?"

David took the paper and wrote down the information while they chatted. Then David left for home, agreeing to see Ezra the next day.

06

The 2ⁿᵈ Key: Reason / Purpose

THE DAY WAS clear, the sky stretching in bright blue azure, endlessly in all directions. For a fall day, the warmth felt good, broken by the occasional autumn breeze.

David followed the directions, driving along an empty state route until a building appeared, with clean black lines and big glass windows. A sign by the road proclaimed the motorcycle brand the dealership sold.

The parking lot was filled with motorcycles. Chrome, leather, handlebars, colors, choppers and more. Cruisers with big, elaborate handlebars, as well as motorcycles ready for a road trip–to go cross country, to enjoy the wide blue sky for days on end.

David pulled into a parking spot and walked in. A stark white interior with a gray tile floor greeted him, with motorcycles sitting on the showroom floor.

A man wearing jeans and a faded shirt with pearl snaps walked up to David. He had a long beard, dark brown but white at the bottom. His hair went everywhere. His eyes crinkled at the edges, as if he were always laughing. "Hiya! What's up?"

David smiled, and said, "Hi, um, is Ezra here?"

"That's me! Are you David?"

"Yes. Regina sent me."

"David! Yes, she told me. Welcome!"

David looked around the dealership, taking it all in.

Ezra waved David over. "Never you mind the dealership, there are other people here for the customers. Let's go sit down."

Ezra led David to a lounge area with a couple of deep leather couches. "Come on, sit down . . . tell me, what have you learned so far about the 5 Keys?"

"Well, Regina started me off, telling me what the 5 Keys are. Then yesterday, Eddie told me about giving. That's all I've got so far."

"Okay, okay. What happened to your head?"

David touched the bandages. "Serendipity, I guess." David told Ezra about the car accident. How he resolved to learn about the 5 Keys To Greatness quickly because of a potential issue.

"Funny how that works, isn't it?" Ezra asked. "When our whole life is in front of us, and nothing is wrong, we can't be bothered. But when something catastrophic happens, or even the threat of disaster, all of a sudden we frantically try to change the things around us." Ezra laughed grimly. "Why wait for bad news? Why wait for that diagnosis?" He shook his head slowly, and continued. "I understand, I guess, but I don't get it, you know? That people only notice the important things when they're about to be lose them." David nodded, as Ezra continued. "You're here to learn about the next key, right?"

"Yes."

"Well, it's quite simple. Simple to understand, harder to put into practice. I guess they're all like that.

"The second key is Reason, or purpose. You want to have a defined purpose, a defined reason for living. Deep down, this is what we're all looking for, for things to be meaningful.

"We want to find meaning and purpose in our lives. If we don't have it, we flounder, we drown, we lose hope. By defining a reason, a purpose to live and work, we can align our lives more honestly."

"How do we find a reason?" David asked.

"I like to recommend defining a reason for each

major area of your life. For most people this is their personal life and their work life. For some, there may be one or two additional areas. But don't pick too many areas of life. Simplicity is important. The simpler it is, the easier it is to hold on to and create lasting change."

"So I pick a reason to live, and that's it?"

Ezra laughed. "Yes, you pick, but no, that's not it. Look, the first step is to pick something, to start aligning your life and your choices with the reason you pick. As you clarify what your reason for living is in more depth, you can change it.

"This is the most important thing, that your reason is not set in stone. You can change it whenever you want. This doesn't mean pick a new purpose every day, or even every week. But as long as you know you can change it whenever you want, it takes the pressure off choosing.

"You can re-align whenever you want, so don't worry about picking the perfect reason. Just pick something, and as you learn more about your purpose in life, realign it."

"Okay." David nodded. "But what's my purpose in life? Or how do I define my purpose?"

"Great questions! I like the second question better than the first. Your purpose in life can be multi-faceted. But how you define your reason, that's talking with purpose.

"First let's discuss your reason for going to work. It's easier to deal with, so we'll cover that, and then delve into your reason in your home life. Many people come to work on Monday morning already talking about going home on Friday. People joke, 'Is it the weekend yet?'

"Imagine, instead, you had a reason for going to work. A deeply satisfying, life-changing reason. You would look forward to being at work. You would want to create lasting change in the world with your work. You would want to help the people around you.

"If you can create this new attitude, and align everything you do at work with this purpose, it would free you. Now every moment at work is another moment you are fulfilling a life lived with purpose. We crave purpose. Everything we do with purpose transcends time and space, helps us do amazing things.

"Let's talk about defining your purpose at work. In every business, at every job, there is an underlying theme to what you are doing. When you pinpoint that larger purpose to the business, you can align your work purpose with that.

"If you change jobs or careers, you can evaluate your new job or new career. Find the underlying theme, then align with that."

David looked confused. Ezra continued, "We'll do

examples in a second, don't worry. Now, the underlying theme may not be the answer every time. You may have to align an aspect of your job with your personal goals. But whatever you pick, realign everything you do at work with this higher purpose."

Ezra watched David as he processed this.

"Let's talk examples. I work in a motorcycle dealership. I sell motorcycles. That could be it, but it's not inspiring. There's more to it. I help people discover freedom. That's one of the main reasons behind buying a motorcycle. To gain the freedom of the open road, the freedom to go where you want while under the beautiful sky."

"But what about the lifestyle? What about the image that comes with buying a motorcycle?" David asked.

Ezra's eyes twinkled as he laughed. "You're right. For some people, this image is part of it. But this isn't how I define my purpose. Don't ever let other people's opinions affect you like that. Your reason is your reason, it needs to make sense to you.

"Another good example? A fast-food worker. A guy working at the burger joint down the road, making minimum wage. Forget about the health implications for now, I'm not suggesting you eat there. What's his reason, what's his purpose? Look for the deeper meaning to what he does."

David thought for a moment. "He, uh, he feeds people?"

"Yes, that's a good start. But let's delve a little deeper. He helps make affordable ready-to-go meals accessible. There are many people struggling with food, in our country and worldwide. He is part of the solution, if he only opens his eyes to the deeper meaning to what he is doing.

"Let's look at another job. You can always find a deeper purpose. Which one?"

David thought. "IT professionals, who work with computers all day."

"IT is support staff. Their larger purpose usually depends on the organization they work for. For instance, if they work for a hospital, then they are helping people heal. If the technology isn't working, the hospital can't function.

"Now let's say the IT worker is part of the administrative staff at a parks and recreation department. That worker is part of the team giving people an enjoyable place for family, rest and relaxation. If the IT isn't working, then nobody in the department can function."

"Okay; what about an accountant?"

"Same idea. If they are an accountant for people, then they are creating the security of knowing their taxes are paid and up to date. If they are part of an administrative staff, then what the larger team is focused on can have a big effect on their purpose in life. If they want."

"Salesperson."

Ezra smiled. "What they're selling, and to whom, dictates that purpose. Selling cell phones? Their purpose is helping people communicate freely. Selling makeup? Their purpose is helping people accentuate their features to find the best image of themselves. Selling insurance? Their purpose is helping create peace of mind for people.

"But think about it. Let's say you sell insurance, and tell yourself that you just sell insurance. Then you would let the people who don't want to hear what you have to say get to you. They would completely affect your state of mind. You're nothing but an insurance salesperson! Nobody wants to talk to someone selling insurance!

"Now shift. You sell insurance. Your purpose, your reason for going to work every day, is to protect people. To give them peace of mind. To make it so they are covered financially for any catastrophic event in their life.

"Now, if someone gets upset at you for trying to sell them? Let it go. He or she is already protected. Or doesn't value the same things you do. No problem. Your reason for working doesn't change.

"And if someone is already covered, you can offer to review their coverage, to help them. Sure, in some ways, it may help sales. If you see gaps in their coverage, you may be able to sell something. But if your authentic focus is to help them, you carry yourself differently. You're protecting people all day long. It changes everything."

"Okay," said David. "That makes a lot of sense."

"Find the deeper meaning behind what you do. Then keep your focus on that. It elevates everything you do in your life. It changes going to work from being a dreary thing you have to do to something infused with meaning.

"It is a work in progress though. You'll see, it can be easy to fall back into the day-to-day grind of life. Periodically, you will want to remind yourself you are working for a larger purpose. It makes it easier to re-center your thoughts to your purpose."

David spoke up, "Okay. That all works, for work. And I understand how realigning helps. But what about life? How do you define a life purpose for yourself?"

Ezra smiled. "Remember, we are not talking about the meaning of life. We are talking about aligning your life with a defined purpose that YOU create. If you want to define your life's purpose as helping more people wear shorts, that's your choice. I can't say I agree with the concept, but hey, it's your life, your purpose, so I would support you wholeheartedly."

David looked at him askew, "How did you know I want everyone wearing shorts?" He waited for Ezra's reaction.

Ezra laughed out loud again, as David joined in. "Nicely done. I always love a good laugh. But remember, we're talking about defining a reason for your personal life now. If you define a purpose for other major areas of your life, the steps will be very similar.

"One more thing. The steps I outline here, these are what I have found to work. The method doesn't matter though. You can use any method you want, any method that works for you. This is the most important aspect of any of the 5 Keys To Greatness. They are your own. Use them however you want. The more you put into them, the more you will get out of them. But use them as you will, make them your own, make them meaningful for you. This can be reiterated time and again. Greatness is whatever it means to you. Use the 5 Keys in whatever way you want.

"You should also know that it's powerful to pick something for your reason and move forward. Getting started on something helps us figure out the right direction even if we start in the wrong direction. By taking that first step to define your purpose, you'll recognize which parts work and which parts don't work. This is why I recommend picking something, even if it turns out to be wrong. Whatever you do, take action. If it doesn't fit, realign.

"Of course, you won't want to realign every other day. But you do want to figure out the best reason for yourself. And getting started helps with that, in my experience."

David stretched his arms, and yawned.

Ezra laughed, "I hope I'm not boring you!"

David laughed. "Nope! It's been a crazy couple of days. I think I need to get up and move around. Do you mind if we walk for a bit?"

"Let's do it. Exercise is important to me, actually, but many people aren't okay with the good old walk and talk." Ezra stood up, went to the counter area. "Want a water or something?"

David nodded, so Ezra grabbed a couple bottles of water. They walked outside and went to the edge of the property. The property beyond was a farm, with fencing at the edge of the dealership's parking lot. Right before the fencing was an area of cut grass, six feet wide or so, that went on and on, in both directions.

"We can stretch our legs here." Ezra started walking on the grass as David joined him.

"You should sit down with yourself and define your

reason for going to work. You can use what we talked about before, or another method. But define a purpose behind your work; what is your driving reason?

"Then sit down and define a larger purpose, a larger reason, for your personal life. It may be harder, but remember, the goal is to pick something. If it isn't a good fit you can always realign in the future.

"As you pick something for work and for home, you start aligning your actions to these purposes. Align the things that you do, and the things that you think, with your defined reasons for living and working.

"Having a purpose creates motivation. You'll see this more as you work to realize your true potential, as you align your purpose with your life. Your larger reason for living will be your guiding post. There will be times when you don't want to do certain things. This is normal. It's okay. But over time you'll see the value in actions that align with your purpose. Even on days when you don't feel like doing it.

"Every new solution, every new creation, requires tremendous personal resolve, perseverance, and more. Knowing the reason why you are doing something helps you focus on the bigger picture. This keeps you moving forward even when everything else inside of you is saying to quit.

"If you need to reach a destination, it's easier to navigate with a compass. A compass tells you if you're on course or not. Otherwise, you get lost. Defining your reason creates direction, so you know when you're on track. And direction helps you feel fulfilled while you are actualizing your life. Of course, writing up long term goals gives you an actual destination to work toward.

"I've found a couple exercises that can help you define your reason, if you like. Use whichever fits you best, or something else.

"The first method focuses on your recurring thoughts. What is the one thought, or the one action, that you keep coming back to in your mind? This is the one thing that haunts you day and night. It keeps popping up, saying to you, 'You should do this.' The one goal that you keep mentally reviewing. It's the one thought that you feel you should accomplish.

"That is one helluva good place to get started. It may not be perfect, it may turn out not to be your driving reason, but it likely will have a lot to do with what drives you.

"The second method I recommend uses three questions. You jot down a quick answer for these questions and then contemplate the answers. You want your gut answer, if possible, so don't think about it too much. Just write what first comes to mind. Then think long and hard about what you wrote down. Those answers should help you define a purpose to guide your life. It may only be the first reason you use, as you refine it later."

They stopped walking as David pulled out paper to write the questions down.

Ezra continued. "First, ask yourself, 'What do I want to be doing with my free time?'

"Second, ask, 'If I could pick only one thing in my life to accomplish, what would it be?'

"Third, 'When my life is over, what are the top three things that I would like to be able to say that I did well? That knowing I accomplished these things would make me satisfied, and perhaps, happy?'"

David scribbled quickly, writing down the questions for later use. As he finished writing, Ezra asked, "Have you read any fiction?" David nodded. "Many books end up dealing with what's called a hero's journey. When you define a purpose in your life, even if you change it later, you are starting on your journey. You are taking that first step to being your best self.

"I've always felt that many of us hide our true thoughts from ourselves in an attempt to make life easier. Paradoxically, these hidden truths actually make things harder and stop us from doing what needs to be done.

"Our life's purpose is one of those things we often hide from ourselves. We stay busy in an attempt to forget about creating meaning in our life. Deep, deep down, though, this is what we crave, this is what we want." Ezra breathed deeply, looking around at the farm, at the woods, at the road.

"Come on, let's head back." They turned around.

"Remember, you'll make mistakes with this. We often have no idea what we really want. I would say it's guaranteed that you'll pick the wrong reason sometimes. You'll realize that you need to redefine your reason again. Don't worry. We're also dynamic; we shift and change as we go through life.

"If you read a book, the characters are often static. They are who they are who they are. You won't see them change during the book. An evil guy will always be evil, the practical joker will always play practical jokes. This holds true for most books; but not always for the main characters. Thankfully, we are not characters in a book. We are living, breathing human beings. We are dynamic. We can change, we can shift ourselves, if we want to and with the right strategies.

"The faster we recognize we've veered off course, the faster we can get back on track. Sometimes, admitting you were wrong is a big step in shifting your reasoning.

"And the life's purpose we are talking about here is not referring to goals. It does not mean to define your life's reason as 'finish college.' That is a goal; when you are finished, you find a new objective and start working toward that target.

"Goals are important. They will make or break you. Use goals! Write them down, actualize them. Create big projects with smaller objectives that break it into more manageable steps! But don't confuse a goal with a reason for living.

"Goals are a part of actualizing a reason, but the reason itself is more of a guiding light. A reason for living could be to create lasting memories for my kids and to be a great dad. This is a living statement. It isn't one particular objective, there are no goal posts to move further and further away. Either you are aligned with that statement, or you are not. If you're creating lasting memories, you're aligned. If not, how can you realign with that life purpose?" Ezra smiled. "That is actually my purpose, for my family and home life."

David smiled and said, "So that's it? A reason I define is something that I'm either aligned with or not?"

"Pretty much. As you go through each day, are the things you are doing in line with your purpose? If not, ask yourself, 'Why am I doing this? Why am I investing my time here?'

"As you answer that, or not, you can pick and choose whatever is best aligned with the way you want to live your life. This refocuses you on your own path to living your own best life.

"Look, work through this once or twice. After

you've put together some initial thoughts, set a reminder to review it in the near future. Explore it again. What are the ways that what you do is about more than you? Is it in alignment? If it is, great; if not, change it." They reached the dealership just as Ezra finished.

"Have you ever ridden one of these things?" Ezra pointed to the motorcycles sitting around the lot.

David grinned, "Yeah, when I was younger. It wasn't one of these, it was smaller. Only three hundred fifty cc's. It was great."

"Do you remember how to shift gears and everything? Want to go for a spin?" Ezra's eyes twinkled as he smiled at David. "When I'm here I love giving people freedom."

David laughed, "So after we talk, you try to sell me?"

"Not quite. I won't push you to buy at all. A ride will certainly help my case. Think of this as a simple offer to reacquaint you with motorcycles."

David laughed again, then declined, citing his head injury. "Maybe I'll come back once I'm cleared."

Ezra nodded, and they walked back to the dealership. David said his goodbyes, expressed his deepest appreciation, and left.

*　*　*

David parked outside Vantage Point. The sun was

getting lower in the sky, creating the golden hour beloved by photographers everywhere.

David walked up to the bar and sat down, waving at Regina when she noticed him. The place was filling up, and David wanted to start heading home before it got too busy.

Regina came over quickly after seeing David. "Hey! How was your time with Ezra?"

"It was great. He tried to get me to test-drive one of the motorcycles."

"Ha! That's his way of saying he likes you. Don't worry, he doesn't try to sell to people I send him. Not to say that he won't sell people I send him, but he leaves sales out of the picture.

"What did you learn? Want to tell me about it?"

"Sure." David nodded as Regina held up a glass. "Just water, please." She put water down on the bar, then put her elbows down, and leaned her face in her hands, staring at David.

"The second key is Reason, or creating a purpose in your life. Having a reason to live gives us a guiding light to apply to all aspects of our life. Ezra recommended defining a different reason for each major area of life.

"Defining the wrong reason is no big deal. I can change my reason at any time. If I find that my reason no longer matches what I want out of life, I can define a new purpose."

Regina nodded, listening to David.

"Having a reason to live, a defining purpose to life, creates meaning in everything we do. Even the most mundane tasks are elevated if we align our life with this higher purpose. Even only eating, if we are aligned with a larger purpose, it becomes a part of actualizing our reason for living."

David drank some water, then sat back and stretched out his arms. "I have to get home though. My wife is supporting this journey, but I can't disappear all the time." They laughed.

Regina stood up, folded her arms, looked at him. "Well said. Okay, tomorrow, please go speak with Celia." Regina pulled out a slip of paper, handed it to David.

David nodded, said his thanks, and left. He headed home to connect with his family, to look through his own life, to define a reason behind it. To define a larger purpose, a focus on the right direction, a guiding light.

07

The 3rd Key: Engage / Presence

A S DAVID EXITED his office, heading to his car to visit Celia, his phone rang. "Hello?" David answered, not recognizing the number.

"Hi, is this Mr. David Harp?"

"Yes, this is he. Who is this?"

"Hi, this is Joni from Dr. Monaghan's office. Is this a good time?"

"Uh, sure . . ." David sat down on a bench in front of his building.

"The doctor wanted me to call you. She wants you back in here at the end of the week for more imaging."

"What did they see?"

". . . everything is still inconclusive. But Dr. Monaghan did stress that you shouldn't ignore this. Can we make an appointment right now for you to come in? Would Friday work? In two days?"

"Ah, sure." David made an appointment for Friday morning. His heart racing, he managed to finish setting the appointment before putting the phone down. He placed his head on his hands, his body trembling in response.

After a few minutes, David felt mostly calm again, and sat up. He took a deep breath and walked unsteadily to his car.

He started to drive though his mind was elsewhere. Distraction took over his every waking moment. He drove automatically, making turns without thinking, ruminating on the call from the doctor's office.

As David drew closer, he calmed down and started to notice his surroundings. He pulled up to a quaint college, with buildings made of stone and hints of gothic architecture. Large buildings rambled along hills, with huge oak trees, maple trees, and ash trees spreading their branches above. The fiery colors of autumn were still visible on the branches. More leaves littered the ground, declaring that time moves ever forward as fall marches on to winter.

David parked his car. He ran up the walkway,

checking his watch, heading to Celia's building. He ran up the stone stairs, through a decorative doorway made of dark-stained wood. The wood and the antique brass showed the wear of thousands of students from the past hundred years.

David ran in checking the paper from Regina again, noting the room number. Checking his watch, seeing he only had three minutes left, he ran on.

David walked up to the room, crossing the polished slate tile floor. Students streamed out of the auditorium. He came closer, waiting for the exiting students to dissipate. When he saw an opening, he slipped into the room, walking down to the lecture floor.

As he descended, he saw a young man wearing jeans and a sweatshirt with a backpack on. The student was talking to a middle aged woman wearing a long billowy skirt. She was wearing a sweater and delicate rimless glasses. Her dark auburn hair was pulled loosely back into a ponytail, but it flowed around her face, escaping the ponytail in places.

David reached the bottom and stood to the side, waiting. The lady looked up as the student said thank you and left.

"Are you David?"

"I am. Celia?"

She broke into a huge smile. "That's me. David, so

kind of you to come out.

"Come, let's get out of here. I love these rooms, but I enjoy the fall, and would like to get some fresh air while we talk."

Celia left her belongings strewn about in a haphazard way. When David looked at her stuff, she said, "I have another class in here soon, don't worry."

They walked up to the hallway and went outside. Celia hugged her arms to her chest to ward off the light chill of the autumn breeze. She started right into it. "You are here to learn about the third key, Engage."

David nodded. Celia smiled. "I'll do my best. There is so much to cover, so many ways to think about it. I'll focus on giving you enough information to work through this on your own.

"Have you ever felt like your life is just passing you by? That you are moving through life, only half-experiencing it, missing things?"

David paused, then nodded, still preoccupied with his earlier phone call.

"Are you okay? You seem distracted . . ."

David took a deep breath. "Ahh . . . well . . . ehm . . ." David stalled, initially not wanting to talk about his problems. "Oh, what the hell. Yes, I'm distracted, sorry."

David told her about the accident, the doctor, and now the phone call. As he spoke, Celia saw the cuts and bandages on his head. When he finished, Celia looked at him. "And you're still learning about the 5 Keys To Greatness?"

David nodded. "Regina suggested it. If I only have a little time left, I want to make the best of it."

"What a noble pursuit." Celia smiled. "I'm actually glad you're learning about this key when you are so distracted. Engage is another way of talking about presence of mind. Of being present in the present moment. And here we have a wonderful opportunity to practice these skills when it can really help you." Celia's smile broadened. She looked up at the blue sky, the clouds mixing with the bright sun, creating a feeling of hopefulness all around.

While still looking into the sky, Celia stretched her hands out, and started spinning slowly. She breathed deeply, in the moment, ignoring David. David watched her in silence.

"Come here," she said, grabbing his hand. They walked to a bench by a small copse of birch trees, with their thin, smooth, silvery trunks. They were overshadowed by the large oak, maple and ash trees, but in this space, it worked. The back of the bench was close to two of the trees.

"Here," Celia said, leaning on the back of the bench, facing the trees, patting the spot next to her. "Let's sit here. Bring your mental self to me, and this moment, for a little. Try to focus only on what I call your attention to. Let's do a short exercise." She smiled. "Don't pay attention to me, focus only on the tree.

"I know you have a lot on your mind. But do your best. If any other thoughts pop up in your mind, let them go. Bring your attention back to my voice and this tree."

She continued, her soothing voice bringing David into the moment, helping him focus on the tree. "Look at the tree. Really look at it. Do you notice how smooth the bark is? Now feel it, use your fingers, and then your hand. What does it feel like?

"Now look up at the branches. What do you see? Don't tell me about it, just look. Experience it, see it. You are not taking a picture. You are experiencing the tree. If other thoughts show up, let them be, let them float off into the distance. Forget about your other thoughts. Focus on the tree in front of you.

"Good. With your hand still on the tree, close your eyes. Take in a slow, deep breath. Hold it for a moment . . . Let it out slowly. Wonderful." Celia continued giving him instructions. Urging him to focus only on the tree in front of him, to focus only on the moment before him. After a while her voice trailed off, leaving David in his own head. He was breathing better, experiencing the tree. David felt less distracted as he pulled back to center.

All was silent. After a while, Celia rubbed his arm. "Are you feeling better? Is your mind racing less?"

David took one more deep breath in as he opened his eyes. He looked up at the top of the tree then took his hand off the tree trunk and put it in his pocket.

"Yes . . . wow. Thank you. What was that?"

Celia smiled at David. "I'll cover it later. First, let's talk about presence." They returned to the path, starting to walk around the campus.

"Many of us are busy, busy, busy, all the time. We run from one responsibility to another with no time to think. No time to interact with the things around us, not even with ourselves.

"Many of us add to this problem by ruminating on what we're most scared of, dreaming up worst case scenarios. We scare ourselves until the thoughts are debilitating, taking over our lives.

"Our minds keep moving and moving, running through thoughts non-stop. If someone thinks about barbecue grills, it can spawn a whole thought trajectory of barbecue grills, especially if you are not paying attention to your thoughts.

"Now imagine someone in a situation like yours. There might be something wrong. Probably not, but it could be a problem. The mind circles around the same thoughts, over and over and over again. Imagine someone is in a bad situation. He tells himself a story, let's say, that his cousin is out to get him. Or that he hates him. These thoughts can then circle, again and again. Especially as he finds things that seem to confirm his story.

"Some of what I am talking about now may share similarities to the next key, positivity. But you can also protect yourself from thoughts circling the drain of your mind by being more present."

They got to one end of the quad, turning onto a path that stretched across the entire lawn. "When we first started I asked you something." She looked at David. "Do you ever feel like your life is flashing past you, and you're barely a part of it?"

David thought for a moment, then nodded. He said, "Yeah. There are times when I wonder how so much time went by since the last time I thought of something. Sometimes it's weeks, sometimes months. I see where I am right now, and I'm shocked to realize that it's so long from whenever I'm comparing it to. It feels like years flash by in an instant.

"The worst of it is, sometimes I feel like I'm missing memories that I should have. Where I feel like I was barely there."

"Yes!" Celia smiled. "Yes, this is what I mean. We want to recognize this feeling and hold on to it. This way we can do something about it. If we are not engaged in our own life, we lose out on all the magic happening around us. Many of us are stuck in the future, or the past, making us miss out on the present.

"When you are fully in the moment, these issues are less of a problem. Yes, time still flies. I don't think we can do anything about that. It isn't part of my research, that's for sure." They laughed.

"Everyone has moments in their life when they were one hundred percent there. Interacting with the world around in a here and now state. Not in the future, not in the past, but here. Now. No worries about the past, no worries about the future, just focused on what is happening right here, right now.

"The present is a present, so treat it that way. Bil Keane, the cartoonist who created Family Circus, similarly said, 'Yesterday's the past, tomorrow's the future, but today is a gift. That is why it is called the present.' It may be cliche, but it is true. The present moment is powerful.

"Being in the moment is like being in a meditative state. It channels all your thought power into the moment in front of you. You enjoy the present moment more. A life lived in the present is a life well lived."

Celia looked at David. "How often are you in a moment, but focused on the past, or the future?"

David nodded as he recognized how often that happened.

"When we are thinking of the past, or the future, we lose the ability to be fully present in the moment. There is little point in ruminating on things we did, what we said, what we might have done differently. Not being in the moment also opens us to making more mistakes. Thinking of the future is no better. Thinking and planning for the future also pulls us out of the present moment. If you are always in the future, there is no present moment. These people completely miss it! They may know what they are doing in five, ten years, but they have no idea what they just did. All because they are focused on a time and place that is not here in front of them.

"I'm not saying you should forget the past, or never think about the future. This isn't healthy either. I always say, 'Regret not the past, but learn from it.' We can learn so much from history, including our own! But by only thinking about the past, or the future, we are never here. We are never engaged with the world around us. This makes it hard to move forward.

"Dedicate time to plan for the future. Review your past to learn from it. But do it willingly, do it with presence, and be fully in the moment. Don't keep a running dialogue in your mind of your future plans, keeping track of all the things you will do 'one day.' Who says one day will ever come?"

Celia sighed and continued walking alongside

David.

"Being fully engaged, being present in the present moment has many benefits. It creates wellness in both physical and mental health. I could go into study after study showing how good it is for the brain, but this isn't the time. If you're interested, you can research mindfulness and presence on your own." Celia laughed. "For now, let's talk about it more practically."

Celia stopped and looked at David. "Take a deep breath with me." She put her hands by her sides, closed her eyes, breathing in. She raised her hands with her breath, breathing in long and deep, using her hands as a guide for her body. David tried to mimic her movements. She exhaled. Celia opened her eyes. "That was a good start for you." She patted his hand. "Come on." They kept walking.

"Have you ever gone to a yoga class?" Celia asked.

"No. My wife goes."

"Okay. I urge you to try it for yourself. Check with your doctor first, of course. At a yoga class, the instructor reminds participants to focus. Focus on your body, on where you are, on your breath. To leave everything else outside of the room. This is presence. This is being in the moment. It means forgetting about your to-do list unless you are looking at it.

"There is a whole technique on this you can look into. There are free online courses and other resources.

Dr. Jon Kabat-Zinn developed it in 1979 and then improved it over the years. It's called mindfulness-based stress reduction, or MBSR. It is one way to explore this concept in detail. Remember, the 5 Keys are open to integration with other systems—make it your own.

"Mindfulness means being fully engaged in the moment to achieve this presence. For some, giving it a fancy name like mindfulness makes it inaccessible, or too new-agey. So I don't like to call it that. Just bring an awareness into the present moment. That's it." They turned a corner on the path.

"When's the last time you did the dishes?"

David paused. "Uh, over the weekend?"

"Were you thinking about other things? Or were you focused on the dishes?"

"Um, I don't remember."

Celia laughed. "Fair enough. But doing the dishes is a simple, repetitive task anyone can use to enter a meditative state. There are other things like it, for example, sweeping or vacuuming. Bring yourself into the moment, and think of nothing else. And use it as practice to bring the same presence into the rest of your life.

"Let's jump back to what we did by those trees. All I asked you to do was focus on nothing but the tree. To bring you away from your thought patterns and refocus your attention on what is in front of you. And as you brought yourself to the moment, you brought yourself back to center, as we say in yoga.

"Call it whatever you want, this centering. Just focus on leaving the chatter in the background. Andy Puddicombe, who wrote Headspace, talks about learning meditation as he tells his story. He learned an important distinction from one of his teachers. Meditation is not about stopping your mind or controlling your thoughts, it is about becoming okay with your mind. It's about being relaxed and okay as your thoughts race by. Like an observer on the side of the road watching cars fly by, it is more about being settled than about being in control. We can't control our thoughts, but we can learn to live with them. As you learn to live with your thoughts, you will stay more centered.

"We jump all over the place in our life and mind. If you think of your life as a line, we are often on one side of it or the other. Too much energy, too little energy. Too much emotion, too little emotion. Too much food, too little food. There are many examples. The main point is that it is best to be in the center." Celia laughed. "Except for anger. I don't think anger has a place in a well-lived life. I learned about this from an ancient scholar, Maimonides. He wrote that it is important to balance every aspect of your life, but not anger. Anger, he felt, has no place in a good life.

"As a side note, his prescription for getting back to center is to swing to the other side of the line. To go to the opposite extreme for a while, and then relax back to center. If someone is impatient, work on being patient to the extreme. Then ease back to a good central point, to a good level of patience." They kept walking, Celia setting a slow pace.

"Until now, we have focused on being present in the moment with yourself. There are at least two parts to this third key, Engage. Your own self, and your social life. Let's talk about being in the present moment in regards to other people. Being a part of the world around you.

"As with before, you can be there or not; it is your choice. You can interact with others and be present. Or you can be in your own head, focused on your own things. But then you completely miss out on the experience of other people. You are going through life but missing every moment of it.

"Humans are social creatures, they need a social outlet. When a human has strong social connections and maintains them, it is powerful and healing. It helps that person weather almost any storm. Being able to fully and completely engage with others can be incredible. The more present you are in your interactions, the more you do for yourself and everyone around you.

"Scientists continue to study the benefits of strong social connections. Studies continue to show people are happier and healthier with stronger social connections. We are talking about increased happiness, a better sense of well-being and more. It lessens stress and sharpens cognitive skills, including memory. Social connections help people live healthier lives." Celia stopped and held her hands up to the sky again. She called out, "I mean, who wouldn't want those benefits!?" She spun around, hands out like a dancer, then continued walking. David marveled at her freedom.

"This is a problem throughout modern culture. Have you noticed that places to be social seem to be disappearing? Businesses have break rooms that are less focused on people sitting together. There are fewer areas to sit and socialize. And of the areas that exist, people use them less and less. It is harder to be social now than in the past and we are all hurting because of it."

Celia pointed at a new bench by the path, sitting by itself. "Thirty years ago, the donors would have made sure it was two benches across from each other. Maybe two benches making a corner. All to create a place where people can easily sit and talk with one another. Now? It's a solitary bench. Hard to have a conversation or sit with friends.

"There are many reasons for this. Smartphones and social media haven't helped. People think they are being social on social media. They're not. I remember when those networks were introduced. They were a gimmick, fun, a place to interact a little online. Now many people would rather spend time alone on a device, claiming to be social. In reality, they are sitting alone and scrolling through other people's lives.

"It is a documented fact. Mindlessly scrolling through other people's lives will make you feel worse about your life. But I'm not here to attack social media." Celia laughed. "Maybe I should be. Though I'd rather focus on the benefits and the value of being engaged with the present moment.

"There is little most of us can do to change all of society. But we can influence those around us. We can be a tiny light in a sea of darkness. One way to help this is to set up our homes and offices to make it easier to socialize.

"You can create little social havens at home. You can invite people to interact by making areas ready for socializing. Make more seating areas, or make sure seating areas are free and clear. Have you ever been to someone's house and the couch is filled with junk? Not a very inviting place to sit, right?!" Celia laughed. "Nobody wants to contend with junk. Even just magazines. Get a coffee table, or a side table. Put the magazines, the books there. Don't make people fight with clutter to sit and be social.

"You can get chairs or other furniture for your backyard, your patio, or deck. Make a place for people to sit. Then you'll feel more comfortable inviting people over. Who wants to invite people over when there is nowhere to sit?

"When you create places to socialize, people use them. Without an area, they get awkward. People don't know where to go or what to do. This leads to less interaction between people, or none at all. This is a big issue for people everywhere.

"We owe it to ourselves to be fully engaged and present at any moment. Think about it. If you are halfway in three different places, are you truly anywhere? Not a single person or project is getting the proper amount of attention.

"While talking about being distracted, let's discuss phones for a minute." David glanced toward his pocket nervously. She laughed. "Yes, smartphones."

She continued. "Try to get in the habit of putting your phone completely away when you're with people. That alone can help tremendously. Part of the reason we are rarely present is because we are wrapped up in our phones. The first second we have an opportunity to look at our phones, we are tapping away. It is messing with our attention span, our dopamine reaction, our ability to socialize, and more.

"Smartphones are taking over our lives. People get smart and joke that smartphones make people dumb. There is truth to that statement. Smartphones hurt our ability to remember; why remember when you can write it down in your phone? They hurt our ability to savor the moment; instead, we want to take pictures. They harm our ability to fully socialize with other human beings when we let them take over our actions. Now most people pull out their phone when left in an awkward situation with another human being. Gone is that moment when people can connect. Gone is any chance for serendipity. People are losing the ability to read social cues. They are no longer comfortable around other people. Our phones are supposed to connect us to the world. Instead, our phones are making us feel disconnected, day in, day out.

"I'm not telling you to get rid of your smartphone. Personally, I did. And I leave my dumb phone behind often, to reclaim that time for myself. If you get rid of your smartphone and switch to something more low key, it would be a big help. But I get it. Many people run their a business or maintain their job via smartphone. So don't get rid of it if you can't. Just be more mindful. Be aware of when you have your phone out. Leave it behind sometimes. Turn the ringer off.

Don't check it when you're bored. Together with friends? Put the phone down. Having a heart-to-heart with your loved ones? Put it down. Taking a walk for quiet reflection time? Leave your phone in your car.

"Many might argue about the music on their phone, the camera, whatever feature they think they need. Well, you can download songs and put your phone on airplane mode. You can also turn off all notifications, gaining the discipline to not check it. It's even better to have it on airplane mode.

"If you switch to a basic phone for a while, it may make it easier to break the smartphone habit. You may rediscover how to be social. Going to the opposite extreme can help you land back in the middle. At least according to Maimonides." Celia sighed.

"Humans are social creatures. We need a human connection, not a phone connection. The more time a person spends alone, the greater the risk for depression. Even without depression, loneliness leads to a lower quality of life. Nowadays we can be surrounded by people but be lonelier than ever. That's the gift of a smartphone.

"Make the decision to bring you, all of you, to life. You can be present, talk to the people around you–no phones. Be fully engaged with people, so you grow and gain from every interaction.

"You look old enough to remember a time without

smartphones. These poor kids today, can you imagine not knowing how to interact with people without a phone in your hands? There are millions out there who don't know how to carry on a conversation. They don't know how to inquire about someone's life. They don't know how to check if someone is feeling bad unless it's on social media." Celia trailed off, shaking her head with empathy for all those lost souls.

They continued walking in silence, now in their second circuit around campus. Celia closed her eyes briefly, took a deep breath, and continued. "There is something else important to a good life. Most people don't recognize the need, but it is there. Play is integral to a well lived life, and it is part of being present in the moment.

"There are many ways to satisfy this need to play. The important thing is that you do it. Dr. Abraham Maslow, the father of the hierarchy of needs, said that, 'almost all creativity involves purposeful play.' When we allow ourselves play time, we relieve stress, we de-escalate. We can introduce playfulness into anything we do. It gives our brain time to process things. Then it's easier to come up with that creative solution."

"What kind of play are you talking about?"

"Well! There are many different types. Use whatever works for you. There is a whole underground culture of board gamers. There are all the classic card games. There is word play, whether on paper or verbally jousting with someone. Robert Fulghum, the refrigerator philosopher, has a delightful essay on verbal play. He talks about playing with complete strangers; people are either in the game or out. You can also do things like Sudoku, word jumbles, puzzles, anything."

Celia shook her head. "It's sad, really. In our society, playing is basically socially unacceptable at a certain age. It's frowned upon. Why? If play is so helpful to us, and research continues to suggest that it is, why shun the benefits of play?" Celia sighed. "Just find a way to reintroduce play into your life. You'll feel better about everything."

Celia looked at her watch. "Oh, my class starts soon." She smiled. "Let's cover a couple more things. When the walk takes us back by my building, I have to go in." She kept walking.

"We spoke earlier of balance, and of the importance of being present with both people and yourself. The goal is to strike a balance between interacting with people and interacting with yourself. It is exhausting spending all of your time with others, or spending all of your time with yourself. You'll want a balance. This doesn't mean fifty-fifty, it means that you feel balanced.

"Remember to spend time with yourself as well. As

long as you are mindfully, spiritually, mentally, or emotionally present, do it!! But make sure you are truly present. A nap is spending time with yourself, but won't unlock the benefits of being fully engaged. You aren't present, you're sleeping. Read a book, take a walk outside. Watch something beautiful like a waterfall or a sunset. Reflect on life by yourself, or lie down and watch the clouds. Do something that you will enjoy and be fully present in the moment. It will allow your mind to process things in free-form."

Walking along the path, they approached Celia's building, the original copse of trees visible in the near distance. Celia continued. "I would be remiss if I didn't add laughter. Laughter is important for your mind, body, and soul. Scientific studies continue to prove this. Now, you can fit laughter into one of two keys. This key, Engage, due to the in-the-moment nature of laughter. Or you can include laughter in the next key, Amazing, because laughter helps unlock the positive aspects of your life. Put it wherever it makes the most sense to you.

"The main point is to find things to laugh about. Laugh with your kids, if you have any. Laugh with your spouse, if you have one. Laugh with your friends, family, and others. The need to laugh never diminishes, but our focus on it certainly does. The more attention we give laughter, the better off we are. Laughter is all-important."

Celia trailed off as the two reached the copse of trees near the entrance to Celia's building. They paused. Celia looked at David.

"Earlier we sat with those trees, and got back to center. You can do this on your own, anytime, anywhere. You can go for a walk in the woods, or in a local park. Almost anything will work if you let it. Leave your phone in the car, if you can. The goal is to spend time with yourself. You can walk in the comforting enclosure of nature, allowing yourself to contemplate life. Or you can allow yourself to be. If you find your thoughts drifting, especially if they drift to the future or the past, bring your mind back. Notice the things around you. The birds, the water, the path, the trees, whatever is around you.

"You can also use the trees or plants as a focal point for light meditation. This is a little of what I was doing with you before. I've heard of a new program out of Japan doing this, called shinrin-yoku, or forest bathing. Research continues to show its efficacy at helping relieve stress and so much more. I've never been to a session personally, but my understanding is that you go into a forest and bathe yourself in the full sensory experience. You bring your full focus, your full attention, to what is around you.

"You can do what we did earlier on your own as

well. Go find a spot in nature. Use an object of focus, such as a tree or a rock. Sit down and experience your focal point for as long as you can. Feel the texture. See the shapes, the colors, the details. Tune yourself into the sound of the world around you. Smell the object, or the air, to see if there is a scent afoot. I would usually stop short at tasting it." Celia laughed. "I'm all for experiencing things with your five senses, but licking a tree or a rock doesn't sound like a great idea. At least to me." They laughed together.

"One great mindfulness exercise you can use anywhere is with fruits or vegetables. When you are eating something, do it slowly. Focus on the entire experience. It changes everything. You can touch, taste, smell, see, and listen to the fruit while you open it, cut it, or whatever. An orange is great for this, because of its bright color and tangy citrus smell."

Celia trailed off. They stood facing each other by the door to her building. She held his hands, looked into his eyes. "David, everything will be okay. Work the keys. You'll discover your destiny. Trust the process. Okay?"

David looked into Celia's earnest brown eyes. He nodded. "Okay. Thank you."

Celia stretched out her arms, enveloping David in a big hug. She whispered, "It's going to be okay." She stepped back, gave David a final farewell, and walked into her building to teach her next class. David walked to his car, thinking all the while.

* * *

Regina stepped outside when David showed up. She leaned against the outside wall of the bar, while David leaned on the hood of his car.

"How was it with Celia?"

David grinned. "Fantastic. I had no idea there are so many ways to fully engage with the world. I've been thinking about what she said the whole way over here. I'm realizing that we only hit the tip of the iceberg."

"How do you mean?"

"Well, the main concept is to engage, to be present in the present moment. And yes, Celia did break it down to being more present with your own self and being more present with others. Self and social, I believe she called it.

"But I realized this concept of being more present applies to everything. We can always be more in the moment and focused on the things around us. Even when doing the most mundane tasks, we can be distracted or we can be mindful."

"This is true. Many people miss it and remain distracted. They can't focus their attention, and then their attention dissipates." Regina paused. "Have you ever chopped wood?"

David shook his head.

"When you chop wood, to split it, you need a solid base underneath. This keeps the force of the axe concentrated in the wood you're splitting. Otherwise, a lot of the force gets distributed into the dirt that your wood is sitting on. This means you are working hard without getting results. You are allowing your work to spread into the ground. It's a waste of effort.

"The same is true for our attention. If we allow our attention to be pulled in a few directions at once, the force of our attention dissipates, just like the force of the ax. Then we can't gain from it in the ways that we should be able to.

"This is why being present is so important." Regina smiled. "Look, I get it. Distractions are everywhere. Most people around us seem fine with always being distracted. That doesn't mean we have to live like that. We can make the choice to live fully engaged in our own lives. Even when you aren't passionate about something. You can elevate the most mundane things by being present."

David nodded, soaking in her words, allowing what she said to settle in as they finished the discussion. Then David got back into his car, heading home to his family. Before leaving, David grabbed his assignment for the next day. He would visit Malcolm to learn about the fourth key of the 5 Keys To Greatness.

08

The 4ᵗʰ Key: Amazing / Positivity

DAVID DROVE DOWNTOWN to find Malcolm. He found a parking spot, left his car, and walked to the busy pedestrian way by the water. David started looking for the crowd that was his marker for finding Malcolm. He walked past the cement structures, passing the landscaped areas. Everything was manicured to be people friendly; nothing allowed to grow rampant, to grow wild, the way the world likes.

As David walked, he saw a crowd in the distance sitting by a concrete amphitheater. He hoped this was the spot. David walked up. People sat around while a man talked to them from the center. He was speaking to all, mixing in jokes. Everyone was enjoying themselves.

David thought back to the description Regina had given him. 'Talking to anything that moves, but with a magnetic energy that draws people to him, like flies to a lamp.' This might be his guy.

The man stood with his dreadlocks hanging down, a deep magnetism felt throughout the air. As David sat down near the back to wait, the man looked at him and said, "And who 'dis, then?"

"I'm David. Are you Malcolm?"

"Ooohhh, he David. He David. And he wants to know if I'm Malcolm!!!" The crowd laughed. The man was talking with a huge grin on his face, both enjoying the moment and joking around. "Well, I want to know who David IS, know what I mean?"

"Regina told me to find Malcolm. I thought it might be you." He stood up. "If not, I'll keep looking."

The man opened up his arms even more. He laughed, loud and clear. "That's the magic word! 'Regina.' She's the one. I'm Malcolm. This man, he must be learning just like us. Sit down, man, I have a few more minutes, then we go and talk."

Malcolm stood there, still talking, still joking. "This mindset, this positivity mindset, it makes all the difference in the world. Take our friend David here; what if he walked up here using his negativity mindset? Maybe he would have dismissed us. Thought, that can't be Malcolm. Then he would have spent the rest of the day wandering around, hoping to find me." Everyone laughed, including David.

"This is an amazing way to view life. Think back to a time when you viewed a situation with a negative outlook, and then you did. Negativity literally shuts us down. It closes us off, it limits our possibilities, it increases the darkness in our lives. It hurts the situation we are in, it hurts us, it hurts everything.

"Now think about positivity, about viewing a situation in the most positive light. When we think about things with positivity, when we put that spin on it, think about it–positivity is expansive. Positivity opens us up, broadens possibilities, and increases the light we experience in the world. Viewing life as amazing literally opens up all possibilities.

"Okay, I know you all have to get back to work. I'll leave you with one quote, and then let's meet up again next week. We'll go into the openness of positivity in more detail. The quote to think about is from William James, an educator at Harvard at the turn of the last century. He said, 'the greatest discovery of my generation is that human beings can alter their lives by altering their attitudes.'" People gave a light clap.

The crowd stood up and quickly dispersed, small groups heading in different directions. One man hung behind to ask Malcolm something. David approached Malcolm as the man left. "What's the deal with that?"

Malcolm laughed. "Look, I have all this extra knowledge because I've been working on myself. I want to share it with the world. Remember, the first key is Give. What better way to give than to spend some time helping people live more positively?"

"Makes sense," said David. "Do you teach them the 5 Keys To Greatness?"

"Ha! I wish. Have you ever heard the saying, 'stay in your lane?' It's about keeping to what you're good at. My main strength is positivity. I mention the 5 Keys here and there. When people want to learn more, I point the way. But any positivity these people bring to the world helps."

"That still sounds wonderful. How do you find the people?"

Malcolm laughed again, a deep, belly laugh, a laugh that begged those around to join in. "The real question is, how do they find me? I started doing this a few years ago, once a week. Just to see what would happen. New people show up all the time. I don't know how they hear about it. I don't tell anyone, but someone must be spreading the word." Malcolm sat down on the concrete bench, near where David stood.

"Yeah. Makes sense." David nodded, sitting down near Malcolm.

"Okay!" Malcolm said, slapping his knees. "Regina sent you here to learn about the fourth key, right?"

David nodded. "I've been working through the keys this whole week. I met Celia yesterday."

Malcolm's eyes flashed briefly, more a gesture of infatuation than anything else. "Oh, Celia, she's something, isn't she."

David laughed. "She certainly seems so."

Malcolm nodded. "Let's talk positivity. Or as it's referred to in the 5 Keys: Amazing. Everything is amazing when you look at it with positivity."

"Okay," said David, nodding.

"You heard the last bit I said before, right? Positivity is a mindset, a way of looking at things. If we compare the two, we see that negativity is dark and limiting, while positivity is light and expansive.

"It's amazing. As children, we have this positive outlook where anything is possible. I want to be an astronaut, I want to be a fireman, whatever. We can use our imagination to fly to the moon and back in the blink of an eye as a kid. But we lose this positive outlook at some point. At some point, we grow more cynical. Why?

"With positivity, we want to reignite this child-like fascination. To reignite the ability to think positively about the world around us.

"Humans have a limited ability to focus on things. There are two reasons I bring this up. There are the subconscious filters, and there is the ability to only focus on one thing at a time. I'll explain," Malcolm said, seeing David about to ask something.

"First is the ability to focus on only one thing. We have a limited ability to process things, which we'll talk more about in a minute. But it is hard to be in a state of negativity and positivity at the same time. You can only be in one state or the other. So at any given moment, you are making a choice—a choice to be positive, or to be negative. And I don't know about you, but I know which choice I would rather make!" Malcolm laughed, David joining in, caught up in Malcolm's addictive laugh.

"One example of this singular focus is the fight or flight response. Imagine you are walking through the forest, and you come across a tiger. Everything disappears from your mind except what is right in front of you—the tiger. You may have the worst stomachache. You may have an agonizing rash. Someone could be pointing a knife at you! Everything will disappear until you deal with that tiger growling at you, whether you run or fight.

"I like to use a photographer as a parable. A photographer usually has one camera body, and many lenses. If the lens on the camera is not the right lens for the picture, the photographer will take off the lens and put a new one on. Just imagine you are a photographer. When you're looking at the world in a negative light, switch your lens. Just switch your lens! From a negative lens, to a positive lens.

"Tell yourself to change your vision to change your decisions. You need to pay attention to how you perceive anything. Your perception is your reality. We will get into that more later.

"Now, obviously it isn't quite that simple, just switching a lens. But it is almost that simple. When you catch yourself looking at something in a negative light, look for the positivity. Look for the way to see that event, that interaction, in a positive way. The more you do it, the better off you will be."

Malcolm took a deep breath, as he paused for a moment, then continued. "Now, about our subconscious filters. There are different estimates of the processing power of the conscious mind versus the subconscious mind. People who worked on these theories include the scientists Bruce Lipton and Daniel Levitin. There are different definitions of the terms, and different ways to measure the data processed. The idea here is not the exact number, but the story it tells when you compare the two.

"You have the conscious mind, which is where we

'reside,' if you will." Malcolm put his fingers up in air quotes and laughed. "This is able to process between 40 and 120 bits of information per second, depending.

"Then you have the subconscious mind, which can process many millions of bits of information.

"You have this huge disparity between the two. There is a lot more information that is processed but not brought to our attention. So there is a constant filter, or a constant decision, by your brain, of what to show you and what to ignore.

"The more you focus on an aspect of life, like positivity, the more the brain discards things that don't fit into that view. The brain automatically throws a filter on itself. If this fits in with what the brain knows to be true, it'll bring it to the conscious mind as truth. If this doesn't fit into your world view, the brain ignores it.

"An example of this would be someone who tells an internal story about their life. 'I'm not good enough to get married.' Whatever happens, he or she will focus on the stimuli that reinforce that story. The new interpretation of events is used as a justification for continuing that internal story. The fancy name for this is confirmation bias, I believe. The main point here is what happens. You see something happen, and interpret it in the way that fits in with your current belief. That interpretation then becomes your reality.

"This is why shifting into a positivity mindset is so important. The more that you apply positivity to what happens in your life, the more that positivity visits you. It affects everything you do. The more you focus on positivity, the less room there is for anything else. Slowly but surely you train your brain to focus on the good. And yes, while we won't go into this here, you can change your brain. This has been proven many times over. It's called neuroplasticity, if you want to look into it.

"Negativity is the opposite. Things like cynicism, sarcasm, an attitude of 'that won't work.' The more you allow this negativity into your life, the more you invite these results into your life. When small things fit this negative worldview, it'll show up in your conscious mind as though it is a fact. This is even though it is only an opinion. Your subconscious mind feeds you this data to show you that it is true, whether it is or not. Most of the time, it is only your interpretation of events.

"You can actually change this negativity cycle. One way to do so is through writing. When something happens to you, and it feels negative, you can journal about it. Remember to put a positive spin on what happened. As an example, let's say your car breaks down. You can write about your experience with a positive spin. When you remember your car breaking down later, you'll remember it as positive, instead of negative. This basically primes your brain to change your experience of what happened.

"By interpreting an event in a positive way, you have the ability to change reality. We are talking about tremendous possibilities here! You can interpret an event in any way you want, and for you, that becomes reality.

"Have you ever read any stories about magic? Harry Potter? Lord of the Rings?" David nodded. "In those stories, the characters can do magic, alter reality. But it's all stories.

"This, though? This is real. This is the ability to change your own reality. This is real magic. It won't change the rest of the world, but it will change your world, and that makes all the difference.

"As humans, we are the sum total of our experiences and how we react to those experiences. Your perception is your reality. The way that you perceive what is happening to you, becomes the way things are happening. All because of how the mind filters out what fits into the story, and what doesn't.

"Imagine a woman, who no matter what happens to her, she tells herself, 'this too is for the best.' A lady who finds the positive in every situation. She has the best meals at restaurants, the best jobs, the best boyfriends, the best husband, the best kids. What kind of life do you think she is living?

David smiled. "A good life."

"An amazing life. She's either the luckiest person alive, or she finds the best in every situation. The best meals? She found the positive aspect to the meal and focused on that. The best jobs? She finds the amazing part of the job and talks about it. The best husband? She pinpoints the good and doesn't focus on the bad. She always finds the best part of everything around her. She is creating her own reality of the best ever, by finding the good.

"This is what it's all about. This is the power of positivity. The more you find the good in every situation, the more every situation becomes good. Make the change, so you can change your reality. Focus on what makes our world amazing.

"And it really works. The world that you want to see is the world that you see. Whatever lens you're using to view the world, this is the world that is reflected back to you. If you see pleasant people who want the best for you, that is what generally happens to you. It's as if our interpretation of the world is a mirror that shows us what we truly think of the world around us.

"This is why viewing the good in everything helps create everlasting change. It allows you to shift your entire view of the world. It allows you to literally change your life.

"I will warn you, though, this only works most of the time. Positivity is not a universal answer. One example is a spouse. Focusing on the good and ignoring the bad is fine, but not if the spouse is abusive or something similar. We also can't change the physical rules of the universe." Malcolm chuckled a little, but David saw the laughter wasn't there.

"Growing up, I had a friend who believed he could fly. He climbed to the roof of his house, and jumped off . . . and he flew."

"He flew? Really?"

Malcolm huffed again. "For a bit. And then gravity set in, and he came crashing to the ground." Malcolm sighed. "He's no longer with us." Malcolm slowly shook his head.

"Ignoring the rules of physics will create a rude awakening. So will crazy optimism when the situation doesn't warrant it. You want a good balance between positive thoughts and seeing reality." Malcolm trailed off for a moment, reminiscing about his friend. Then he continued.

"The truth of the matter, is that it doesn't really matter. The truth. It doesn't matter." They both laughed. "It is your interpretation of the truth that matters. Maybe that driver did mean to cut you off. Maybe your family meant to snub you. But you can make the choice to interpret it in the best possible way, making your experience a positive one. Those other people, they live with their internal toxicity. You stay fine though. You continue with your positive mindset and your attitude intact. You harness the power of positivity to change how you experience reality.

"This literally helps you feel better, live better, and think better. Studies continue to explore the benefits of a positive mindset. They all point to the same idea. The more you focus on positivity, the better off you are. This affects everything around you.

"Here is something amazing, by the way. A little thought exercise. Do me a favor, close your eyes."

David looked at Malcolm.

Malcolm laughed. "Trust me, it's only for a minute." David closed his eyes. "Now imagine a picture of something positive. Someone helping someone out, or someone giving someone something they don't need to give. Really focus on this picture of someone doing something positive."

David did so, sitting there picturing helping the lady with her groceries the other day. After a moment of silence, with no further instructions, he said, "Okay, I have it. What now?"

Malcolm laughed again. "You can open your eyes." David opened his eyes and looked at Malcolm, who continued to laugh. "You looked so peaceful, I didn't want to disturb you! I was gonna let you sleep!" They both laughed.

After the laughter died down, Malcolm continued. "There's a psychology professor in North Carolina who researches this stuff. Her name is Barbara Fredrickson. According to her research, now that you did that, you will perform better and you will come up with better, more creative solutions to problems. All by imagining something wonderful!!

"Now think about this. If, by imagining something positive, you create such lasting effects, what happens when you view your whole life in a positive light?" Malcolm finished off this question with his arms held out.

He put his hands down, took a deep breath, and looked at David again. He smiled. "And that's about it."

"I do have one more thing I can tell you, if you like. It's a small exercise that you can use. It will help you see the amazing things already in your life. Do you want to hear it?"

David nodded. "Yeah, I could use something like that. Is it hard to do?"

Malcolm laughed. "Everyone always wants to know if it's hard. Yes and no. It shouldn't take too long, but it can be hard to get started, and it's hard to keep it going.

"Once a day, write down three good things that

happened to you. It may be easiest to anchor this in the evening. But write three things that were amazing, or positive, or even neutral but with a positive spin on it. The basic structure can be 'this is what happened and this is why it was good for me.'

"After you do this for three weeks, review what you wrote. Read your list of things that were good. How do you feel about seeing these? How does this list make you feel internally?

"As you recognize how you feel when looking at this list, you can make a decision if you want to continue. I recommend continuing. This exercise creates a shift in your head so you focus on the positive in your life instead of the negative. It helps you harness the full potential of your mind."

David nodded. The two sat there, enjoying the coolness of the day, the view of the water beyond the concrete. Finally, David asked, "That's it then, huh?"

Malcolm laughed. "Not by a long shot. Regina probably told you that each key is deep. You can delve into it and explore the depth of it as you move along your life. This is a basis for you to build on as you see the benefits of having a positive mindset. The benefits of focusing on positivity instead of negativity.

"As long as you continue to explore these concepts, you will gain. You will get out of it what you put into it. Your clarity will continue to spark the release of more positive energy into your life. And you will continue to bring more positive blessings and joy into your life as well.

David nodded. "Of course. Regina did talk about that. Makes sense."

Malcolm smiled and nodded. He stood up. "Glad to hear. " He looked off in the distance. "By the way, if you run into a Simone, talk to her. Have any discussion with her she is willing to have with you." Malcolm turned. "Gotta go. Good speaking." Malcolm moved into the walkway and slipped away.

09

Happiness and Gratitude

D AVID SAT ON the concrete barrier for a few more minutes, thinking about everything. He couldn't get past Malcolm's parting words. Who was this Simone? Why did Malcolm say that?

David stood up, ready to go see Regina. Then he could go about his day. Tomorrow was the last day of learning about the 5 Keys To Greatness! He was excited about applying the 5 Keys to his daily life. David started toward the street, to where he parked. And then he saw her.

A woman walked toward him, close and getting

closer. She was dressed peculiarly, to say the least. Loose clothing that flowed all around, pushing a shopping cart filled with stuff. David looked, trying to figure out if it was filled with random knick-knacks of the homeless or something else. The lady walked straight toward David. He noticed she veered into an angle that would intersect with his walk if he continued leaving.

David stopped walking. He stood there and watched this lady approach. When she got close enough, she stopped. She looked up at David through her disheveled hair, one eye above the other as her head was on a tilt. She narrowed her eyes, scrutinizing David.

"I saw you talking to him. I did."

David looked at her. "What?"

"I saw you talking to him. Hoo, he's been avoiding me!! You talk to him again, you tell him I'm a-going to talk to him, I will. You talk to him again, you tell him we are overdue for a discussion. Overdue!"

"What are you talking about? Or, rather, who?"

The lady looked at David again, as if seeing him for the first time. "Malcolm. That man you were talking to. We go way back. But we need to talk." She pulled her cart to the concrete benches, starting to set things on the flat surface. David watched for a moment. He realized it wasn't the random haphazardness of someone not all there, but the careful setting of an experienced street vendor.

"Are you selling that stuff?" David asked.

"If I can. Who says people will buy it?" She turned her face to him and grinned. "Why, do you want to look at my wares?"

What David could see looked intriguing. Eclectic, but intriguing. Essential oils, sweaters, select titles of books, boxes of strange-looking soap, and more.

David said, "No thanks, I'm okay. Who are you again?"

The lady cackled, as she continued setting up. "Who am I? Who are you?" She laughed again. "Who are you?"

David cleared his throat. "I'm David."

She stood up, turned, and looked at David. "David, huh? As if that it explains it all." She made a raspberry sound with her lips.

The lady stood, arms crossed, looking at David, until David got uncomfortable. "Okay. Okay, okay. Fine. I'm David, I was talking to Malcolm." She continued watching him. "I'm looking for a better life, to unlock my destiny. I was talking to Malcolm, hoping he could help me along the way."

"That's better, sweetie, now I at least know something." She turned and continued setting up her wares. "I'm Simone, by the way," she called over her shoulder. David's suspicions were confirmed. He felt both relieved and nervous. David sat back down on the concrete, near Simone, while she finished.

"Malcolm is avoiding me, and yet he talks to you. Why?" Simone looked over at David as he sat down.

David shrugged. "I'm learning about the 5 Keys To Greatness. This is one of the stops. I go somewhere else tomorrow."

Simone laughed. "The 5 Keys To Greatness?" She looked over her goods, making sure they were set the right way. "Those are certainly useful. But there is more to know than just those five keys."

"Wait, you know the 5 Keys To Greatness?"

"Yes I do. Oh yes . . . I . . . do. They are helpful. But there is a bit more to know."

"What are you talking about?"

Simone made one final adjustment to the pieces, moved the cart to the side, and came back. "Move over." She shooed David down the concrete, making room for her to sit between her impromptu shop and David.

"Look, honey. We live in the United States of America, during the greatest prosperity ever, or close to it. The greatest prosperity ever. A thousand years ago, rich people would have given half their fortune to have and use what poor people have now.

"So here we are, in this moment of great prosperity,

in which we should all be happy. You would think we could just be happy and enjoy our lives. You would think. Happiness and contentment are so important!

"But depression, despair, and more are at their highest levels. Suicide rates continue to climb. Why? What is going on that we have so much money, so much wealth, so much stuff, but we are drowning in despair?

"So yes, the 5 Keys To Greatness are good and wonderful. But if you don't understand what I'm about to tell you, it's all for nothing. What I'm telling you is almost the precursor to the 5 Keys.

"Go ahead, tell me the 5 Keys To Greatness again. I need help remembering sometimes." David was watching her, which she may have thought was a look. "I know, I know, there is a word to remember them, but it slips my mind sometimes. What are they? Spill it!"

David laughed, a little nervous, and said, "Well, the word to remember is GREAT." David used his fingers to now count off each key as he described it. "The five keys are Give, Reason, Engage, Amazing, and Tenacity. Give is to–"

Simone cut him off with a wave of her hand. "Yes, yes, I just needed the words. Okay. Let's see." Simone looked over, saw David's confusion, and backtracked. "We're going to do a quick review of the 5 Keys To

Greatness to discuss how they help spark happiness. If you are willing to let it in."

"But I haven't done the fifth key yet."

Simone dismissed this with a wave. "Doesn't matter. Doesn't matter. We are talking in brief concepts. Stuff you need to know, but can wait to understand in more depth later. Hang on." She stood up, and stood by a man who was browsing her wares.

After finishing with the man, Simone sat back down next to David. "Okay, let's see, where was I? Ah, yes, to give.

"Giving breeds happiness. Any time we think of others, it creates a cycle within ourselves that sparks more happiness. As long as we remain open to it. You have to allow the joy and the wonder of giving to enter your heart. Giving is one way to bring happiness into your life.

"The next key is Reason, right?" She didn't wait for a nod from David. "Yes it is, yes it is. When we are living a life aligned with purpose, it is harder to be gloomy. It's the people who sense they have a deeper purpose, but are not fulfilling that purpose, who are often miserable. The people aligned with their own purpose tend to not be as sad. There is less time to be down when you are driven by purpose." Simone nodded at David, almost daring him to contradict her.

"The next key, it's Engage, isn't it? To be more

present. Mindfulness helps with happiness, yes it does. If we are always looking at the future and the past, and never the present, it is harder to be happy. The more aware you are of any moment, the more of a capacity for happiness you will have.

"Amazing, isn't it? The next key? To be positive? Do I need to tell you that maintaining a positive mindset helps perpetuate the path of happiness?" David laughed, and Simone went on.

"The last key is Tenacity. Look, I know you're going to go and learn all about it. And you should. But that isn't my point. My point is that too many people want to give up after the slightest friction, after it gets a little too hard. That isn't the way. You must persevere, and move forward. But you'll get into that when you're learning about it. Just realize that there is an element of happiness that comes from a job well done. There is a contentment from completing a project despite the difficulties. Completion is its own reward.

"When you use the 5 Keys, you are more open to happiness."

"Are you saying that if I do the 5 Keys To Greatness I'll become happy?"

Simone laughed, slapping her knee. "No, boy, no way!! It's never that simple. I am saying if you focus on these keys, and open yourself up to being happy, each key can help you unlock happiness. But you must let it.

Each key can be used to increase happiness, create more joy, help you be more content with life. You still have to discover your own happiness. You still have to let the good feelings in. Nothing will take you there all on its own.

"This leads me to my next thought. Happiness is important, but so is gratitude. In fact, gratitude helps breed happiness most of the time. If you focus on what there is to be grateful about, you open yourself up to more blessing. It's all because you appreciate what you already have.

"If you only add one thing to your life, let it be gratitude. Add gratitude in any way you can; thank more people for the little things they do. Notice when you can feel appreciative for something.

"Some of the best ways to find the gratitude in your life are to write about it or to involve your family and friends. You can write down something on a slip of paper and keep it in a box, then review it once in a while. You can write about it in a journal or in a diary. Or you can discuss what you are grateful for at meals. And not just at Thanksgiving! The point is to start recognizing all the little things in your life. How they are helpful. Why they are helpful. What gave you that feeling of gratitude.

"As you focus on gratitude, you can refocus your mind to see the things that are good around you. You can better see the wonderful circumstances around you. Get into this habit of being grateful, and expressing gratitude. This will help you find that joy and contentment we've been talking about. And with time, you'll see it in everything you do. Well, in almost everything." Simone laughed. "There will be times that you aren't happy. That's normal. You won't always find joy and contentment in the things around you.

"This is probably a good time to remind you that nothing lasts forever. Happiness, joy, contentment, any positive emotions we spoke about–by their very nature, they are fleeting. They come and go, and other feelings and thoughts and emotions will come and go as well.

"These feelings only make a difference because of other feelings. If you don't have bad feelings, you can't have good feelings. Basically, think of these feelings as the up part of a roller coaster. You can only have an up if you have a down. If you are always up, then it isn't up; it's normal height. You remain on a plateau.

"So appreciate and recognize those times when you are experiencing other feelings, other emotions. Those times are what make happiness and contentment so important, and so valuable. We must truly experience emotions and feelings on both sides of the spectrum to gain from the pleasant side.

"Feel the world around you–both good and bad–so you can truly feel the good."

Simone stood up. She started shifting her things around, tweaking the setup. David watched her for a moment, and started to get the feeling she was done. That she had said what she was going to say, that she was finished.

"Simone?" David asked.

"Yes? Oh, you're still here, are you?"

David laughed and nodded. "I am. I just wanted to say thank you." Simone nodded to herself as David turned and walked away.

* * *

"David!" Regina called out when she saw him. "How was your time with Malcolm?"

David sat on a stool by the bar. "Not just Malcolm, but Simone as well."

"You got to meet Simone? She made an appearance for you?" Regina laughed. "Wow, you are lucky! Want a drink?"

"Water, please." She filled a glass with water.

David took a sip. "I did get to meet Simone. And it was amazing meeting Malcolm. What he has to say about positivity, sounds life-changing. But then Simone came along and I've been thinking non-stop: why are happiness and gratitude not part of the keys?"

Regina smiled, and said, "I'm glad you asked. First, let's look at happiness.

"Happiness is not actionable. I can't tell you to go 'be happy.' You won't know what to do. You won't be able to change anything. That will lead to frustration, instead of good feelings.

"Gratitude is more actionable, and very important. Unfortunately, it lacks the full depth of the 5 Keys To Greatness. It isn't a broad enough category.

"But think about all you've learned about positivity. Think about maintaining that positive mindset. What does it take to look at things in a positive way? What comes out of seeing things as amazing? When you look at it like this, you see that happiness and gratitude fit into the fourth key almost perfectly.

"Happiness is one outcome of maintaining a positive outlook. The more you focus on being positive, the more likely you are to feel and be happy.

"Gratitude is also a form of being positive. You look at things around you in a positive light and see them as a reason to be thankful.

"Does this make more sense to you now? Do you see that happiness and gratitude fit within the fourth key?"

David was taking a sip of water. He put the glass down, nodded. "Yeah, that makes sense. Thanks."

"But while these two concepts fit into the keys, they often apply across the other four keys as well. At least a little bit. As an example, you can give more appreciation. And giving produces more good feelings, leading to happiness." David nodded. "But these are so important, I'm really glad that you spoke to Simone and she pointed them out individually. Happiness and gratitude really deserve a lot of attention.

"I think a big part of the discontent of today is a lack of gratitude. If you can't be thankful for the good things in your life, then you keep expecting more and more but will never be happy. Expectations do not lead us to a good place though. Expectations actually make us focus on what we want, instead of being happy and content with what is. And this leads to unhappiness, despair, mental anguish and more. 'If only things were like this, then I'd be happy.' It just isn't true. If you were happy, maybe things would be like that.

"This concept is based on ideas by the happiness researcher from Harvard, Shawn Achor. He would tell you to create a paradigm shift. Go from the thought of 'when I have blank, then I'll be happy,' to the better method, which is, 'I'll work to be happy.' Only then does success and everything else come to you—but you're already happy."

David nodded, took another drink of water. He looked at his watch. "I've got to get going soon."

Regina nodded, then reached out, wiping the bar. She looked over David's shoulder as a group walked in, talking all the while. "Any other thoughts from your meeting with Malcolm?"

David took another sip, then said, "Yes, definitely. I love the idea that positivity is like a photographer's lens, something we can switch out. From a negativity mindset to a positivity mindset. A switch to focus on the best in everything, even if you don't love it. You find the best part of it, and focus on that, and why it is good."

Regina put out her hand to cut him off. "I want to be clear, though. This isn't lying to yourself, or allowing yourself to be manipulated, or allowing yourself to be taken advantage of, or anything like that. That is not what this is all about. This is about making a conscious choice to view things in the most positive light, when it makes sense. You can see things for what they are, so you don't get taken advantage of, and then find the positive angle that will move you forward."

David nodded. "I also liked how Malcolm pointed out the difference between positivity and negativity. How negativity is dark and limiting while positivity is light and expansive."

Regina smiled, and said, "I've seen this to be true at so many points in my life. I have completely closed off my life to new experiences, and everything shrunk. Once I moved to a positivity mindset, using the 5 Keys, everything opened up completely. New possibilities arose everywhere."

David continued. "He also told me about the

subconscious and conscious mind. About how we create our own cycle of negativity, if that is how we view the world."

Regina laughed. "The negativity cycle. It's a real thing. There is a lot of blessing to gain from opening ourselves up to positivity and the good things happening all around us. No reason to focus on negative things, or to tell ourselves negative stories. Positivity brings about positivity. Anyone who tries it will see it to be true. You attract what you expect. No two ways about it. Rhonda Byrne, who wrote The Secret, has a great line about this: 'You bring about what you think about.'"

David put his glass down, finished his drink. "Oh yeah, that's the other thing I wanted to remember from Malcolm. He had a good line about keeping a positive mindset. He said to change your vision to change your decisions."

"Oh, that one is new! I have to write that down. Hold on." Regina grabbed a slip of paper and a pen. "What was that again?"

"Change your vision to change your decisions."

Regina finished writing. "Okay, thank you! I'm glad you remembered that."

David nodded. He looked at the time and said, "Oh, time's up. Got to get moving." David stood up, thanking Regina profusely. Regina held out the slip of paper that David almost expected at this point. He looked down, saw the name Jade and nothing else, and looked at Regina.

"She'll call you. Her schedule is always a bit up in the air. If she doesn't call you by late afternoon, call me. I'll see what's going on."

David nodded, looked again at the slip of paper, and made his way to the exit. He got into his car, thought about his appointment in the morning. Nervousness arose once again. His stomach fluttered, his blood pounded in his ears. He stopped, took one deep breath after another. David focused his mind on the positive aspects of the appointment. He thought about how it was for his health; with his own best interests in mind. That the tests were only to help him. That it was most likely nothing, and more. Slowly, slowly he calmed down. Then he started to drive, and headed home.

10

The 5th Key: Tenacity / Persistence

D AVID PULLED UP to the doctor's office. It was a lone building, set off the street, an alternating mixture of glass windows and dark brown brick columns.

He put his head down on the steering wheel, grabbing hold with both hands. He focused on deep breathing to gain some calm, some serenity. Despite still being nervous, David got out of the car and walked inside. Time to get imaging done.

"Good morning!" David gave a huge smile to the lady behind the desk. She handed him a set of forms to fill out. David laughed as he thought of a patient, sitting in a doctor's office, filling out so many forms that his problem had disappeared before he finished the pile of forms.

"What's so funny?"

David laughed again, and shared the joke.

The receptionist laughed with him. "Feels like that sometimes, doesn't it?"

David nodded, then sat down and filled out the paperwork. He handed it back to her, then sat in the waiting area, both nervous and calm, waiting for the testing.

Finally David's name was called. He walked to the testing room with the technician. On the way, David passed Dr. Monaghan. She was flustered, papers in her hand haphazardly, threatening to fall all over the floor. Her white coat was askew, her hair out of place. Dr. Monaghan seemed overwhelmed, and it brought to mind something interesting. David wondered how the 5 Keys To Greatness would help Dr. Monaghan with the stress of being a doctor.

"I'm glad you made it in so quickly!" said Dr. Monaghan. "Like I asked Julie to tell you, it's almost definitely nothing. This is out of an abundance of caution."

David nodded. "Understood. I'm still pretty nervous! But I want to be here, in this world, so here I am."

Dr. Monaghan looked at David. "You seem incredibly calm. What's your secret?"

David laughed. "I don't feel that calm! Though I'm sure I'm more calm than I would have been a week ago. I've been learning about a remarkable program. I think it's helping."

Dr. Monaghan looked at David, slowly nodding her head. A nurse poked her head out of a room and called to her. She turned and rushed down the hall.

The technician led David into a room. The machine inside looked almost like a spaceship, with a small chair between a few huge objects. The technician told David to keep his head perfectly still the entire time. The tech situated David in a seated position, and then went into the other room.

"You good?" The technician asked through the intercom. David held up a thumbs up, and the testing began.

The noise was almost unbearable, loud beeps and blips and more. David was forced to sit in one place for nearly an hour. Despite the noise, David was able to remain more in the moment than he would have been capable of previously.

Finally, finally, the noise stopped. The technician walked into the room, and helped David off the chair. The two walked through the office again. David made an appointment to return in a few days, and then he was free.

David's phone rang as he sat down in his car. He looked at it, and didn't recognize the number. "Hello?"

"Hey, it's Jade. David?"

"Yes. Perfect timing, I just finished."

"Oh, good. We're supposed to meet up today. I thought we would go on a hike nearby. It'll illustrate the point really well. Plus I love to go there. Wanna pick me up?"

"Sure. Where do I go?"

Jade told him how to get to her. David drove to her street and honked. She came out, climbing into the car holding a small backpack. She told him their destination, and the two started on their way.

Jade pulled on her seatbelt. David noticed she was very skinny, but pretty in a girl-next-door sort of way, with exotic looking features. Nothing specific but definitely striking.

"I'm so glad to see more people learning about the 5 Keys."

David grinned. "I'm only trying to better myself. Regina said it well, trying to live my best life ever."

Jade nodded. "That makes sense. Deep down I think we're all trying to get as close to greatness as we can before we die." She paused, watching the passing scenery. "Have you gone through the first four keys?"

David nodded. "I did. I finished the fourth key yesterday. You had great timing when you called, I was just finishing an appointment."

"What kind of appointment?"

David hesitated. He thought of all the people who already knew what was going on. He realized so far it was helping more than hurting to share it. So he told Jade about the appointment. He told Jade about sitting in the machine while they did the tests. How long it felt and how hard it was to sit there, but he powered through and stayed to the finish.

David stopped talking while Jade laughed and clapped her hands. "Well done, man, well done! I'll get out of the car here, it sounds like you've got this under control!"

David glanced at her. "What are you talking about?"

"First of all, I'm joking, so don't get so worried." Jade chuckled. "I am here to tell you about tenacity, about persevering when you don't always feel like it. And you started off your day doing exactly that!"

"I–I guess you're right. I did do that." David grinned, then thought for a moment. "But that can't be all there is to it, can it?"

Jade laughed. "In a sense, yes, just power forward and keep going no matter what, and that's basically the entire idea. When it makes sense. But we're going to explore it in more depth. You're stuck with me for a while longer!" Jade cackled playfully.

"Let's start with belief. Belief is the currency through which we purchase achievements. If you don't believe you can do it, you will not be able to do it. It may be self-sabotage, or something else. But you need to believe you can accomplish something to make it possible. It is this very belief that opens us up to accomplish the things we need to do in life."

As they drove into a wooded area, Jade gave David more specific directions. He turned onto a smaller paved road, driving next to a river now, through trees, heading up.

Jade continued. "Think about belief. Have you heard of John O'Leary? He was badly burned as a kid. The doctors gave him a zero percent chance to live. Zero!! He should have died!

"John lay in the hospital after it happened, bandaged all over, the worst yet to come. He asked his mother for reassurance, 'Mom, am I going to live?' All he wanted to hear was that it will be okay! She recognized that it would take a miracle, a huge force of will, for him to live. So she asked him, point blank, 'I don't know, do you want to live?' This forced him to make an active choice–do I want to live, yes or no? In making that choice, John made the choice to persevere. To persist despite all odds.

"But think about it! Without that choice, that

conviction, that belief, he may never have made it! It is through our belief that we are able to accomplish." Jade pointed at a parking area, "Right there, you can pull in right there."

David pulled the car into a spot, then looked around. They were in the middle of the woods, in a hilly area. Trails headed off from the parking lot in a few directions.

"Come on!" Jade got out of the car, bringing her pack with her. "I have water. Let's go."

Jade led David to a trail that led downwards. They walked down the trail together, while Jade continued. "We should touch upon fear, even though it isn't the perfect opposite of belief. Fear is difficult. Fear can be both a positive message or a negative message.

"Sometimes fear is telling us to push through and move past. That what we face is a good thing, a time for growth. Other times, fear is telling us to keep away from something." She laughed. "The wisdom is in knowing the difference.

"When you get a bad feeling in your gut, when you are about to do something that doesn't feel right, that's often fear telling you to keep away. That feeling that it may not work out well is a warning. Keep away from it, don't do it. Many people have gotten into trouble by continuing despite this feeling. If they listened to their gut, they may have stayed out of trouble.

"Sometimes, though, it's a new project, or something new to learn, or somewhere new to go. In these cases it's probably good for you. If the fear kicks in then, you need to power through the fear. You need to experience it and move forward anyway. Doing new things is how we grow. We don't move forward without trying new things. If you want to achieve anything in life, you need to try new things. You need to challenge yourself." Jade continued downhill, along the path. David wondered how they would get back up.

Jade continued. "You need to break yourself out of your comfort zone. You need to move past it, challenge yourself, and grow. If you find a comfortable place and stay there, you will remain stagnant. You will never move past your preconceived notions. It takes effort to grow, to achieve more with your life.

"Think about every single thing we have in our lives now. These are things that the people of yesterday fought for years ago. If they had given up halfway, we wouldn't have these things. From things like women's suffrage to the civil rights movement, to inventions, medical treatments and more. Every great change happens because someone was willing to continue past all reasonable limitations. This persistence unlocks incredible gifts to all humankind.

"In school we learn history, along with the names of people who did incredible things. Who accomplishes these crazy, world-changing acts without perseverance?

"Think about the people along the paths of history who affected great change in the world! You can love them or hate them; they lived in a different time and era. It is hard to judge someone's actions without recognizing the social construct and culture of their times. The main point is that none of these things would have been finished if the person behind it gave up halfway through." The trail they walked along followed the river, on its way down the hill. Now it turned away, continuing its path downwards.

"The examples are innumerable. We learn the names of the people who persisted. We learn their names because they stayed the course and discovered great things.

"Thomas Edison and the light bulb is one of the most famous examples, 'I learned a thousand ways to not make a light bulb.' Joan of Arc, who fought against tyranny and is remembered across the end of time. Mother Teresa, spreading love and acceptance throughout the world, despite difficulties. Christopher Columbus discovering America. He may have never found funding if he did not remain persistent. The founding fathers of the United States, standing up for what they believe in, persisting despite great costs in human life and more. Certainly doubt crept in, but they kept at it. Winston Churchill with his uphill battle, his war he was forced to wage against an unbeatable enemy, Nazi Germany. Churchill kept at it and saved the world. Abraham Lincoln. He persevered, staying true to what was necessary. Lincoln and the rest of the Republicans kept at it, eventually giving freedom to every slave. Even though, in the end, it cost him his life. Martin Luther King, Jr., fighting for peace, for equality, for more, despite the hardship. He must have felt the futility of it all at times, yet he continued. It cost him his life as well. Rosa Parks fighting against segregation. The steps she took were surely terrifying, but necessary."

"I could go on, and on, and on. These people were up against insurmountable odds. There were times these people felt there is no point, I can't keep going. When they felt they must give up because there is no way forward. But move forward they did! Persist they did. They continued, despite how little progress they seemed to be making. Despite how much they felt inside there is no way that they can do it. They applied tenacity, persistence, and perseverance to their life. We all gained, as the world is a better place now than it was before they started."

They reached the end of the trail. As the trail turned a corner David saw a waterfall. He looked at the waterfall, following its path upwards, watching it flow, basking in the noise, the beauty.

"Beautiful, isn't it?" Jade asked.

David nodded, slowly, still catching his breath, enjoying the view, speechless for the moment.

"When you're ready, I have something else to show you." Jade sat on a rock to watch the waterfall. She pulled her backpack onto her lap, pulled out two bottles of water. "Do you want a drink?"

David nodded, and took a bottle from her. He was a little out of breath, but feeling better. He drank deeply.

Jade slowly unscrewed the top to her water, took a sip, and continued. "It's also a consistent theme among writers. An author submits a book to publisher after publisher, agent after agent. They all say no. Then the book goes on to win an award. One such example is A Wrinkle In Time by Madeleine L'Engle. The agents and publishers denying these authors are just doing their jobs. They deal with hundreds or thousands of submissions in a very short time. We can't fault them for doing what they think is best. At the same time, you cannot let someone else's judgement of you become your verdict. He or she is not judge, jury and executioner. Why would you give someone that much control over your life?"

"People all over will be naysayers. They'll tell you, you can't do this, you can't do that. If you believe them, you allow them to control your life. Why in the world would you allow their opinion to affect your reality?

You don't need to let it affect you! It's only one person! How can you let it get you down?

"If you listen to the naysayers, you allow their negativity to change your life for the worse. Why give them so much power? Besides, their negativity goes against the fourth key!" Jade took a long drink from the open water bottle in her hand.

"How are you doing? Ready for more walking?" Jade laughed as David looked at her like a deer caught in the headlights. "We're very close. Think you can do it?"

David took another drink, and nodded. "Sure, if it's close."

Jade smirked. "Not saying you're out of shape, but if you move around more, you do better when going on hikes. Just saying."

David laughed, recognizing the joke in her tone. "I won't deny it, I could get out more. It'll be harder on the way up."

Jade laughed. "Yes, but we'll take more time on the way up. I also brought snacks. It helps the body stay in peak performance when exercising. I won't go into the scientific details. But if you plan on doing endurance sports, look into nutrition for long-distances." She brought David closer to the waterfall, navigating a path up the side. It was a little steep, a little slippery, but not technical. They managed fine.

"You do a lot of endurance events?" David asked.

"I've done events here and there. A couple of marathons, a few multi-day bike rides. Endurance events are a great way to learn your breaking point. You definitely learn how to apply persistence to your life. I'll tell you more about that soon. First I want you to see this." Jade continued, getting closer to the falls, off to the side.

Jade looked around. "Here it is!" Jade called out. She put her pack down, and took a seat at a rock, watching the falls. "Look around. Do you see anything fascinating?"

David walked over, a few feet from Jade, looking around. He saw the waterfall, cascading down from above, pouring gallon after gallon of water down the cliff. Water breaking up in the boulders below, continuing the cascade down. He saw the trees, a mixture of evergreens with ash and oak trees, interspersed with plants, stones, and more. He saw the rocks, slick with water from the spray of the waterfall. David noticed a little drip, drip, drip, of water in the corner, falling from above onto the rocky formations below. David saw the green sheen of the mosses growing on the rocks, creating a stunning emerald landscape. David noticed the river below, where the water from the waterfall endlessly ran to join. David saw the stream, flowing on and on.

David took a deep breath, feeling the stress dissipate

as the scene around him imbued him with a sense of calm. "I see a lot of things that are fascinating. Everything here is stunning. What are you trying to bring my attention to?"

Jade laughed. "Valid point. Okay. In that corner, go look, and tell me what you see." Jade pointed to where the water dripped down a drop at a time onto the rocks.

David walked over to watch the drip, drip, drip. Suddenly he noticed that where the drips of water hit the rock, there was a round hole. "Is this what you are talking about?" David called to Jade.

Jade clapped her hands and laughed. "You've got it now! That's why we're out here. What lesson can you learn from that?"

David watched the water dripping down, drip, by drip, by drip. One drop of water fell at a time, one minuscule drop, yet here was a hole in the rock. A space carved out in a hard substance, from something soft like water.

David turned, looked at Jade. "The water is making a hole in the rock. Water is light and fluid, even soft, yet it is making a hole in the hard, unforgiving rock."

"But why is it making that hole? What is allowing the water to penetrate the rock?"

David looked again at the steady dripping. "Is it because the water doesn't stop?"

"Whoohooo!!" Jade threw her arms up in the air and yelled. "You've got it. The water doesn't stop. No matter what, it keeps dripping. We may think that there is no way that water can penetrate stone. It doesn't seem strong enough to break into stone. But that steady dripping is enough to make a hole in stone. Over a great period of time, the water creates this hole. It is the very fact that the water doesn't stop, that it keeps on going, drip after drip after drip, that creates this hole.

"If water dripped on the rock a thousand times, there would be nothing here! You wouldn't notice anything once it dried off. But when the dripping is incessant, when it doesn't stop, when it continues, day in, day out, at some point you get an indentation. And then you get a bowl. Eventually, the water creates a hole. If enough water is flowing for long enough, you get stunning landscapes like the Grand Canyon.

"This is the power of persistence. This is the power of tenacity. Sometimes we push forward, to make something happen. We want to change something about our life. But it feels like we are getting nowhere. It is the exact same thing as the water and the rock. The progress we are making can be so small, so infinitesimal, that we don't notice we are moving forward. We won't notice how far we have come. Then all of a sudden, we see the shape of the bowl cut out, the hole forming in front of us. From that point forward all of our progress is easy to see. This is only possible because we kept with it, day in and day out.

"Just stay the course, keep the destination in mind. Focus on the outcome and keep moving forward during the long, hard moments. This is how we change the world like those people we spoke about before. We change the world because we are changing ourselves. It's hard to see how much we've changed while in the moment, when we are focused on ourselves. This is when you should remember the water and the rock. Remember that your steady, persistent dripping will work slowly at the rock of your habits to create the change you so desperately seek. Create the new world that we all wish to see.

"This is what tenacity, the fifth key, is all about. Applying perseverance to the things we do, to the things we're passionate about, to our actions. It creates a profound effect on our life."

Jade rummaged about in her backpack, pulled out some snacks. "Here, eat something, we'll head back whenever you're ready." She walked over to David.

"I'm not that hungry."

Jade laughed. "It isn't about being hungry. It's about giving your body the fuel it needs to operate. Remember I mentioned endurance athletes before?"

David nodded, reluctantly taking a snack. He sat

down on a rock, in full view of the waterfall, and started eating.

"Endurance athletes are a great example of the power of persistence. I told you I did a few events. Nutrition is an integral part of being able to do these events. You must eat. People who don't eat, or aren't eating properly, don't make it. If you don't give your body what it needs, you can't take the next step.

"Now think about if we switch out food here for tools. You must give yourself the tools to be successful or you will never get anywhere. If you don't have the tools to be successful–the fuel to do so–you won't achieve what you want.

"Tools can refer to anything. As we said before, belief is a big one. If you don't believe you can run a marathon, as soon as it gets hard you give up. Because you don't believe you can do it. It is so different when you have a deep inner belief that you can do it. If you start running a marathon with a deep belief in yourself, even if you haven't trained properly, nothing will stop you. It will get harder with every mile, yet you will keep moving forward. The closer you get to the finish line, the more torture you will feel. But as long as you believe you can do it, you will push yourself and do it.

"I know this first-hand. I was not really prepared for my first marathon. I didn't know how hard it would really be. I started going and felt the full brunt of the craziness of what I was doing by mile nine. That was almost the farthest I had ever gone, with over sixteen miles still to go.

"By the time I got to mile twelve, I wondered why I signed up for this. At mile fifteen, I was officially in unmapped territory. I had never run more than fourteen miles before. I was ready to quit. I could feel my entire body rebelling against me, and I almost gave up on myself. But I thought about that finish line. I thought about all the reasons I had deep within myself to start this journey, to end this journey, and I kept moving forward.

"While I was running I went through every reason I should quit in my head. In the end I pushed those thoughts out of my head and held on to every reason I should keep going. At some points it was so bad that I couldn't think of a single reason to keep going. My body felt like it was falling apart. My nipples were raw from rubbing against my jersey. In order to continue, I pushed everything out of my head. The pain, the exhaustion, the doubt. I pushed it all out of my head and kept my inner sight on that finish line.

"At around mile eighteen, the discomfort melted away. I don't know why that happens, but it does. People talk about endorphins, or runner's high. I don't know what it is, I just know that when it hit me, I felt great again. I was still exhausted, still in pain, still not okay, but the immediacy of everything dissipated. I focused on putting one foot in front of the other, taking one step at a time. I kept pounding out those feet, those yards, those miles. Just one more step, and then a little more. That's what being persistent is all about. It's about keeping the goal in mind and moving forward, one step at a time.

"I crossed that finish line. I was miserable and crying by the time I got there. I was ready to quit for miles and miles. But I kept pushing. No matter how hard it got, I kept going. And I made it. Every. Single. Step. Every. Single. Mile." Jade took a deep breath.

"Tenacity is a consistent theme with endurance athletes. Endurance sports are more of a mental challenge than a physical challenge. Of course there is a physical aspect to it. The real test, though, comes when you feel like giving up. Many people tell themselves they could if they wanted to, and then quit. Marathons, biking one hundred miles, called a century, completing a difficult triathlon. Every endurance event requires an incredible amount of self-belief with an attitude that says I'll make it, no matter what.

"And nature! Here we are out on the trail, I've got to mention thru-hikers. These are people who start at one end of a trail and hike straight through. They'll often do a famous trail like the Pacific Crest Trail or the Appalachian Trail. Only sheer determination helps them get to the end. It is months of hardship. The people willing to give up when it gets tough are similar to the people in life who never end up making it. Giving up on the journey means giving up on your goals and dreams. Those who decide that I am finishing this, and I am doing it no matter what, they do it. They finish. They earn the satisfaction of a huge accomplishment.

"Think about mountain climbers. A mountaineer needs everything it takes to summit; the mental, the physical, the sheer force of will. He or she can be in great shape. It still takes intense mental fitness to push the body to its breaking point and beyond. To bring oneself to the brink of despair and then say, just one more step, and then, to say again, just one more step. A little bit more, now a little more. It is sheer madness sometimes, but often, madness is needed to separate the winners from the losers. It is this tenacity that gives mountaineers the glory of climbing the mountain and surviving to tell the tale.

"It is that magical, frightening moment, that we need to pinpoint. Recognize it and then move past it. That moment, when everything inside, when everyone around you, says to quit, to give up, you can't do this, that's the moment you must stand up, you must dig deep within yourself, and make it happen."

Jade saw David was finished with his snack. "I can

take the trash." David handed her the wrapper. "Come on, you ready to hike out of here? We'll probably need a few breaks on the way." Jade laughed. "It's basically all uphill."

They started climbing down from the falls, to get back to the trail. David asked, "What about when you don't feel it is the right thing to continue? Like when something isn't the right fit? Sometimes you start something and then realize it's not within your life goals. Do you still have to continue in the face of all adversity?"

Jade laughed. "The idea of tenacity is not to trap you into everything you start for the rest of your life. The goal is to continue with things that are important to you, even when you feel like giving up."

They reached the bottom of the falls and started back on the trail toward the car. It stayed level for a while, but David could already see the trail rising in the distance.

Jade continued, "Look, I get it. I do. You'll start projects thinking it's what you want. Then you realize it doesn't fit into your life goals at all. That it is taking time away from the things you really need to accomplish. There are many examples of times when applying tenacity would be counterproductive. Persistence is not always the answer.

"But our minds are fickle beings. The brain can

convince itself of almost anything, including that you don't want something even if it's best for you. Get outside guidance from friends, family or associates. A sounding board is usually helpful, because these people can help you see the right answer. But remember that there are times that others won't see the truth that you see." Jade walked silently for a minute.

"Did you talk about balance with anyone?"

"Yes, with Celia."

"She's good at that. This is another example of applying balance. Persistence and tenacity are all-important, but if you apply it equally to everything in your life, it will consume you. It won't be helpful. If you direct perseverance at the right things though, you will be unstoppable. You will run up proverbial mountains, conquer them, and then go straight to your next mountain, and conquer it; over and over again. All through applying tenacity to the right things, in the right way."

The two were breathing hard now, as they made their way up the hill. David pushed himself as long as he could, following Jade's lead. Then he wheezed to Jade, "I'm stopping! I need a break!"

Jade laughed and turned around. David saw she was breathing hard as well; not as hard, but out of breath. She noticed his surprise, and said, "Well, what do you expect? We're going uphill." She breathed out loudly.

"Uphill is tough no matter who you are. But I'm glad we stopped.

"First of all, I have an exercise for you, if you want. When you have a few minutes, reflect on your life with paper and pen in front of you. Think about the past. Write down three times in your life when you used persistence. Times that you went on and on despite great hardship.

"Once you've pinpointed your three moments of tenacity, write up the outcome. Write up how you felt afterward, how it affected your life; was it good, bad, or neutral.

"If the three moments you pick turned out for the best, this will reinforce the power of persistence for you. If these didn't have positive outcomes, you can use the fourth key and spin it with positivity. In any case, it should be easier applying persistence to your life in the future.

Jade looked up the hill, then back at David. "Are you ready to keep moving?"

David nodded; some of his breath had returned. The two were about to start. Jade put out a hand to stop him. "Wait! Wait. I had an idea." Jade turned back to David.

"You remember earlier I told you about my first marathon?"

"Yep!" David said, still breathing harder than

normal.

"Well, one thing that always gave me extra energy was what some would call visualization. I pictured myself running the entire event. I imagined putting in the effort to cross the finish line. I watched myself being the inspiration, the hero, I wanted to be at the event celebration. After playing those videos in my head over and over again, my energy levels went right back up.

"We talked about belief before." David nodded. "Well, belief ties into this as well. By creating a visualization of what you want, you give your mind, body and soul clarity in what should happen. And make it happen you will, once you believe.

"I could go into all sorts of new-agey stuff about this. But usually the best teacher is experience. So I want you to try this, right now. We still have a ways to go up the hill. Realistically, we may have to stop one or two or more times to finish this uphill hike."

David laughed. "That's all?"

Jade smiled. "Close your eyes . . . picture hiking all the way up the trail with ease. See yourself reaching the top of the hill. Feel the healthy exertion that lets us crest that climb. Now you can see your car in the distance. Your car symbolizes triumph. Your car symbolizes victory. Once we get to your car, you are finished with this hike."

David's breathing slowed, he felt calmer. Jade noticed his changed demeanor, and went on. "Visualize that moment. You haven't done anything like this in a while. Picture yourself hiking again, up, up, up. Knowing you can hike down, and then back up, is liberating and intoxicating. You are a hiker now.

"That moment, when we get over the top of the rise and see your car, is the moment we've been waiting for since we walked down. It is when you overcome; it is the moment you prove to yourself that you ... can ... do ... it."

Jade took a deep breath, and drank from her water bottle as David drank as well. "Shall we?" Jade asked with a smile. David agreed and they continued hiking up the trail. This time David was in front, setting a healthy pace. David bounded uphill, finding foot holds in the rocks and the roots, staying focused on what lay ahead.

Before long David burst through the end of the trail and into the parking lot, without a second break. David emerged triumphant, Jade seconds behind him. She had a huge grin on her face, as she watched the power of visualization once again. David threw his hands up and shouted, "Wooooooo!!" Jade laughed, her laughter turning into a cough as she tried to catch her breath. "You okay?" David asked. She nodded. David shouted triumphantly again and laughed as they walked to the car.

"Come on, let's get going." David said as they got into the car. Both still a little out of breath, a little sweaty for the effort, despite the chill.

"How was that?" Jade asked. "Not so bad, huh?"

"That was amazing! And that was all from this visualization thing you told me about?" David pulled out of the spot, and started driving.

Jade laughed. "Visualization is not everything for everybody. It is not the end-all be-all. You still have to do the work. In fact, if you only visualize the result without perfecting the work, you'll lose motivation instead of gain it. Your body gets tricked into thinking you already did it.

"But when you need to be mentally tough, visualization can give you an extra edge. You can use imagery to bring you to the brink of success and push you over the edge. You can see yourself doing what you need to do to get what you most desire; then you'll have the stamina to turn it into reality.

"Some people may tell you that visualization is everything. They'll say that all you have to do is visualize a victory and it will come true. This is somewhat true, but it can be deceiving. You do need to believe in anything you want to happen. You must believe it is possible. But you also need to put in the work. You need to make it happen.

"Some people swear by visualization. It could be they are using it in the way we spoke about here; visualizing the work, not the results. It could be other things as well. For many people, as they visualize something, they make small tweaks to what they do. This helps actualize the change they wish to make. Remember, as Durant paraphrased Aristotle, 'we are what we repeatedly do.' If visualization helps you put in the work, if it helps you invest the repeated effort to create results, fantastic. Have at it, do it as much as you need.

"But if you think that visualizing an outcome will change your life, without allowing it to influence what you do . . . well. I think you'll have a rude awakening when nothing is materializing for you. You need to do the work to make the dream work. That's just life." Jade took a long, deep breath, her discourse apparently over.

David drove silently, absorbing all she said. "You're saying to visualize, but don't expect visualization alone to change anything."

"Yes. What's the smartest investment strategy?"

"To diversify."

"Right. Don't put all your eggs in the same basket. Same thing here. Visualize, believe you can do it, but also put in the hard work. You need to do the work to create the reality you want."

David's phone rang. He picked it up on the car audio. Regina asked if he was still with Jade, then explained that she wasn't at Vantage Point. David would have to come by another time to wrap up. "Make sure you come visit me over the next few days. You don't want to wait too long!"

"Jeenz, baby, I can hear you." Jade called out. "We haven't stopped talking about things. David will still come find you one of these days, right?" Jade looked over at David, who nodded.

"Okay, good. How you feeling today, Jade? You okay?"

"Right now I'm okay. Getting out into the woods always helps, you know that."

"Oh, I know. I'm so glad you got out. I really have to get going though. Try to do a short review! Bye now, Jade, hang in there! Feel good!"

Jade and David both called out good-bye as Regina hung up.

"So, David, let's do a little review like she asked." Jade teased. "Tell me some things you learned while we were out."

David cleared his throat. "Let's see. The fifth key is tenacity. It's all about remaining persistent in the face of adversity.

"I noticed three big themes while you were talking. Belief, fear, and keep moving forward. Belief is what you need to do anything. If you can't believe that you can do it, you won't be able to do it. Fear often indicates that we are about to grow in leaps and bounds. To uncover this, you need to move past your comfort zone even if you are afraid to do so. Unless you're breaking the law. Then stay well within your comfort zone." David smiled at Jade, who returned the smile. "Lastly, you have to keep moving forward. Wasn't Walt Disney known for saying that?" Jade nodded. "You said endurance events teach us to sometimes forget everything else, to keep placing one foot in front of the other. To stay persistent, take just one more step.

"I definitely appreciate that trip to see the water and the rock. I love the visual. If water makes a hole in rock, with a single steady drop, then we can move worlds with persistence."

Jade drank some water as they pulled back into the city. Their trip together was over. "That was really well done . . . oh, that's it over there, make that right . . . this building is perfect, thank you!"

David stopped the car to let Jade out. "Thank you. That–that was amazing. The hike was tiring, but wonderful. It's been so long since I've been on a long enough hike to get some exercise." They laughed. "The waterfall was beautiful. Thank you for sharing that. I'll have to show it to my family."

Jade turned to David and smiled. "The pleasure is all mine. Persistence is one of my greatest strengths, but also one of my greatest weaknesses."

David started to say something, to ask Jade about this, when she unbuckled her seatbelt and lifted her backpack. While picking the backpack up, she snagged a bit of her hair in her hand. Her hair shifted noticeably on her head. Jade's eyes widened for a second. She gave David a brief smile, with so much sorrow, so much hope, that David was speechless. Jade got out of the car.

"Really, thank you." David called to Jade. She looked back down into the car. David could see one silent tear trailing down her cheek. Her bittersweet demeanor was strange, after her pure optimism the whole day.

"It is really, and truly, my pleasure. Make the most of your life. We only have the one." With that, Jade gave David a small wave and walked off. Down the street, toward home, or wherever.

11

The Doctor Again

DAVID SAT IN the examination room, nervous, waiting. The morning outside was bright, cheery, not a cloud in the sky. David took a deep breath, focusing on the good things in life. David tried to focus on what he could control and to let go of all else.

Dr. Monaghan flew into the room, her coat trailing behind her. She held David's chart in her hands, looking through it. She put down the chart, pushed her glasses up. She looked at David, and then remembered something. "One more second," she said, rushing out of the room, leaving the chart behind.

A few minutes later she walked back into the room. "I'm sorry, I left this behind." She held up a manila envelope. "These are the results from your readings."

"Good. What's the verdict?"

Dr. Monaghan smiled. "I'm happy to tell you that it's good news. With everything we saw, this last round of imaging was a precaution. Sorry to have to call you in like that, but I like to be sure."

David nodded. "I understand."

"Everything we saw in the hospital must have been an aftereffect of your accident. At this point, I am as certain as can be that you are in the clear." She laughed. "You're going to be okay."

David exhaled loudly. He put his hands over his face, and breathed.

"Nerve-wracking, isn't it?" Dr. Monaghan smiled.

"Yes. Yes it is. I know it was probably nothing, but I–I've still been nervous the whole week."

"I completely understand. I've always thought it might be fun to pop a bottle of champagne when it's good news. Say congratulations, have a little celebration." She smiled. "I don't think I could get through the day drinking that much champagne though." She laughed.

A nurse poked her head into the room. "Dr. Monaghan, we're ready for you in room three." She left.

Dr. Monaghan looked flustered, looking around to grab things and move to the other room.

"Hold on," David said.

"What?"

"Hold on. Take a minute."

"What do you mean? I have to go."

"Dr. Monaghan. You just gave me my life back. Take a minute. Be happy about it. Celebrate! Enjoy the moment!" David stood, held his arms out. "You're rushing from patient to patient to patient, paying attention to everyone but yourself. Take a second, enjoy the wonder of the moment!"

Dr. Monaghan looked at David cautiously. She sat down, dropped her eyes. "You–you're right. I can't always find time for me." She sighed. "There's a lot of pressure, being a doctor."

She looked at David again. "I don't even know where to begin." She covered her face with her hand. "I've been running, non-stop, from college, to med-school, to residency, fellowships, and now this position." She fidgeted in her seat, stood up. "I have to get going."

David said, "Look, I'm not saying to ignore everything. I'm not saying not to see your patients. I wanted to make two main points. The first is that you should take a moment, just a moment, to celebrate this new lease on life you just gave me."

Dr. Monaghan smiled. "Thank you. Well put. Congratulations on having your life back." Her sincerity showed as she slowed enough to fully appreciate the moment.

David continued, "The second point is this framework I learned about. I think it can help you break out of the cycle of insanity you're in. It's really easy to put into place and it can change your life.

"It won't take too much of your time. Spend some time learning about it. Then you can implement it even while you're busy at work. But it can improve every aspect of your life, if you work the pieces and let it influence you. You don't have to be busy, busy, busy, until it is too late. Until you realize your entire life has disappeared before you had a chance to live it." David paused.

"I've only known about this system for a few days, since my accident. Already it has had a huge impact on my life."

"What's it called?"

"It's called the 5 Keys To Greatness. Do you remember that lady Regina you met at the hospital? She'll walk you through it."

Dr. Monaghan stood, chin in hands, silent for a moment. "Is this what you mentioned last Friday?" David nodded.

A light knock sounded on the door. The nurse

peeked her head in. "Should I tell the patient you'll be there soon?"

Dr. Monaghan nodded. "Just another minute."

The nurse left. David looked at Dr. Monaghan. "What do you say? The best case is that your entire life changes for the better. The worst case is that you spend a few days learning of a new way to look at life."

Dr. Monaghan breathed deeply. "I'm in. What do I do?"

12

Be GREAT: Putting It All Together

DAYS PASSED BEFORE David returned to Vantage Point to talk with Regina. David walked in, late afternoon on Thursday, just before sunset. David was surprised to see Ezra from the motorcycle dealership sitting across from Regina, both of them morose, talking quietly.

David walked up. "Hey guys."

Regina and Ezra looked at David. "Oh, hey, how are you? Glad to see the bandages are off." Ezra stood up. "I'll hang around, Regina, go ahead. Can I grab the billiards?" Regina handed him the set of billiard balls, and Ezra walked off to the pool table, where he started to shoot by himself.

"Everything okay?" David asked.

"Yeah, basically." A tear spilled out of Regina's eye, belying her words. She laughed. "Okay, no, nothing is okay. But let's talk about that later."

Regina came around the bar. "Come on, let's go sit on the roof. Maybe we can catch the sunset."

Regina led David to the back of the bar, where she grabbed her sweatshirt and they walked up the stairs. They went to the table and chairs and sat down.

Regina looked at David and laughed. "Back to where we started, huh?"

"Yep. Here we are."

Regina reached over to the cooler. "Want a beer?"

David looked around, relishing the cool breeze, the sky changing from daylight to sunset, and nodded. Regina pulled out a couple of longnecks, popped the tops and handed one to David. He took a drink. Regina was distracted, looking off into the distance where the sun approached the horizon. She shook herself out of it and looked at David. "Sorry, my mind is not quite here. Let me start over."

Regina drew in a long breath and slowly let it out. She half-smiled. "As you can see, no matter how much you work on yourself, there will still be times when it's difficult to be fully present. Distractions get to us, emotions come up. Our goal is not to be perfect all the time, but to do the best we can.

"Enough about me. Let's talk about you, and your experiences these past few days. Erm, I guess it was last week. How did it all go, learning about the 5 Keys To Greatness?"

David took another sip. "I think this is probably one of the most influential weeks of my entire life. Thank you. Really. And my deepest appreciation to your keyholders who described everything so well."

Regina sniffled a little. "Are you seeing how these five keys are all you need to be exceptional in your own life? Do you see how you can use this framework to easily shape your own greatness?"

"Yes. I love that it is super simple to remember. As long as I remember the word GREAT, I've got the whole system."

Regina smiled. "Oh, don't think that knowing what the 5 Keys are will automatically make wonderful things happen. You still need to do the work."

"Of course," David said, "Jade talked about that." Regina looked away. "That's the case with everything, right?"

Regina sniffed back tears and nodded. "Yes it is. As with everything, you get out of it what you put into it." Regina paused, took a drink. "That reminds me. There are two concepts that will help you unlock all 5 Keys

To Greatness."

"There's more?"

"Not really. Take them for what they are; compatible thoughts. They're easy to remember, but even if you don't remember them, don't worry. The concepts are passion and action. Say it quickly, turn it into a mantra: passion and action!" Regina put her beer down.

"Anytime you want to make a difference in your life, you will need passion. If you are lackluster about something important to you, you get uninspiring results. To get lasting results you need deep passion directed toward a goal, or toward something. Unaimed passion will take you nowhere. You'll continue your lifelong wandering, but passionately, blindly leading yourself to nowhere. You also need to channel it in the right way, toward good, healthy things. For instance, drug addicts are passionate, but not in a healthy way."

David nodded, taking it all in. "Okay, passion makes sense. What about action?"

"You can have a great idea, but without action, it won't happen. It will stay an idea. Even if you aren't positive what you want in life, you need to take action. If you start on the wrong path, you'll see it and correct the course. But if you never take action, you won't see what needs to be fixed. You'll remain where you are." Regina trailed off. "Unfortunately for many, they remain where they are forever." She stared off at the bursting colors of the sunset, going quiet.

Regina sighed, looked at David. "Sorry, I'm thinking of people I know who could use action in their life."

David nodded. "Yeah, I know what you mean."

"Never mind them . . . let me ask you a question. What are we able to tell about the people around us and what they are thinking?"

"Not much, unless the person tells us their thoughts."

"Exactly. Not much. We can see what the person does, make inferences from their actions. But ultimately, we're limited to information about their actions, their clothing, and their mannerisms."

David smiled and nodded. "Sounds about right."

"So while our thoughts are important to us, our actions are much more important to everyone else. Actions are influential on our long-term life. Our thoughts are internal, they help guide our lives. But our actions are external, and affect how we live and feel about our lives. Our actions lend reality to our thoughts in many cases. Actions last. So take action whenever you can."

Regina continued. "Remember, this isn't a miracle system. There is no such thing, unless God has one. This is a simple system that you can use to unlock your greatness within. But passion and action can help you create this change.

"I tell people all the time: if you look deep within yourself, you'll recognize that you already know a lot of this. You'll see the truth of the keys within your heart. Our minds often try to stop us from doing what's best. This framework is all about implementing everything in an easy-to-remember way.

"If you want to see people who instinctually know all or most of the keys, watch little children. You can see kids working tirelessly to solve a problem. One child sees another child feeling sad, and they give a gift to make them feel better. Kids search endlessly for the reason behind everything. Little children are present, engaged, and almost always positive.

"You see, we have these skills. We're practically born with them! As we grow up, the world, cynicism, people, expectations and more conspire to make us forget these things. I don't know why, but I see it all the time. Life happens, we get busy, we forget. But we can use these five keys to focus, to realign. We can regain what we lose in transition from childhood to adulthood.

"Our own true greatness is waiting for us. Waiting, behind a simple door with only five small keyholes. We can launch ourselves on our own way to greatness, as long as we unlock the door, as long as we practice all five keys! Simply refocus your life. Realize that greatness is within your reach, and you can do it."

Regina took a deep breath. She looked back at the fading sunlight, took a drink of her beer.

"Something I may not have mentioned is that the 5 Keys To Greatness are about YOU. These keys are about interacting with yourself to elevate your own life. There's an old African proverb that says, 'if there is no enemy within, the enemy outside can do us no harm.' We are often our own worst enemies, deciding we can or cannot do something with no evidence.

"This is all about you. About self-mastery. About using the 5 Keys To Greatness to better yourself. When you do that, you make a positive impact on everyone around you. This is definitely within reach, but it is up to you to find the focus, to find the time. You can unlock your destiny.

"And other programs, there are obviously other programs out there. You have to find the program that works best for you. That doesn't mean that one program is any worse than the other. Well, some might be." They laughed, Regina still subdued. "Some people like to implement multiple programs. You have freedom to choose, especially with the 5 Keys To Greatness. The 5 Keys are built to work with other programs. Going forward, you should look at any program you want to use in your life to see how it fits into the 5 Keys To Greatness. Most of the time the other program fits entirely into one of the keys, or you'll see that each element of the program fits neatly into different keys. Using the 5 Keys To Greatness with other systems is practically never a contradiction. If anything, it complements anything else you do. Just remember the five words, the five keys, symbolized by the word GREAT, and you will be okay. Give, Reason, Engage, Amazing, and Tenacity."

On this last word, Regina broke into sobs. She put her head into her hands, and her shoulders shook, as she bawled.

A quiet voice said, "How's she doing?"

David turned around. Ezra stood by the door to the roof, leaning on the doorpost, watching them. "I–I don't know. She was on a roll, and then she fell apart."

Ezra nodded and walked over to them. He pulled out another chair, took a beer and a water from the cooler. He put the bottle of water on the table, opened the beer, and held it up. "I want to make a quick toast." Regina kept her head down, but put a hand on her beer. David lifted his beer, watching Ezra. "To friends, to eternity, to dreaming, to persistence, to living your best life," Regina's sobs got louder, "to elevating yourself, to finding the best part of you."

As Ezra finished his toast he walked to a drain, then poured out his beer. Regina, still crying, looked up. Her eyes red, puffy. She picked up her beer. "To Jade." She saw David trying to understand what Ezra did, and explained while Ezra sat down, "He doesn't drink."

David still held his beer, a part of the finished toast. "Fine. But what are you talking about? To Jade?" Regina and Ezra looked at David, exchanged a glance.

Regina asked, "Did Jade tell you why she was our best choice to explain the fifth key to people? What makes her so special for persistence and tenacity?"

David shook his head, slow movements. "She mentioned her endurance events. But with the way you're looking at me, I'm guessing that's not the main reason."

Regina sighed. "No. It's not."

She took a deep breath, about to speak. Ezra held up his hand. "I'll take this one . . . Jade was sick. For a very long time."

David asked, "Was sick?"

Ezra nodded. "As in past tense. Did you notice that she was wearing a wig?"

"There was a moment, a weird movement of her hair, but other than that . . ."

"She often didn't tell people. That's not to say she was hiding it from you, or that she didn't want you to know about her hardest moments. Jade so desperately wanted to be better, she refused to look at herself as sick. And it helped a lot. Her doctors thought she had only a few months left to live ten years ago." Ezra laughed. "Shows what they know. Doctors can be right, but sometimes, doctors tell patients bad news and it becomes the truth. Unless the patient is strong-willed and challenges the doctor's understanding and estimate." Ezra took a drink of water. "I think it was Les Brown, the motivational speaker, who said that doctors shouldn't tell patients they're terminal. Instead doctors should tell patients that their ability to treat that patient has terminated." Ezra sighed again.

"But she was fine on that hike! All the way down and all the way up."

Regina said, "You remember I told you to call me if she didn't call you? She had her good days and bad days. That was a particularly good day, she told me. At least until she got back. The rest of the day was very difficult after that hike."

"Did I–"

Ezra cut him off. "Don't think that for a second. Jade's favorite place to be was in nature. She told me once that if she could, she would grab a backpack and take to the woods until she had no strength left . . . but she had concerns that someone would find her body and be traumatized, or that rangers would suspect foul play."

Regina took over. "That would have been one helluva way to go, huh?"

They sat in silence. Finally, Regina said, "Jade used to say that persistence was her greatest strength and her greatest weakness."

David perked up. "Yes, yes, she said that to me, right as she was getting out of the car. What did she mean by that?"

Regina answered. "Jade used perseverance as a tool to help her stay the course. She did everything she could to regain her health. But some things she did in her pursuit of health didn't help, and they may have hurt. I think that's what she meant by it. I don't know. Perhaps she meant stubbornly holding on to things that were not the right path. Traits we view as strengths or weaknesses are never only that, but are as we use them."

Ezra said, "Recently Jade told me about something she read in a book by Pedram Shojai called The Art of Stopping Time. It bears repeating now. It's called the Time Garden. We can view life as a garden that we're growing. Each plant we are tending to is an aspect of our life. The more time and attention we give to one aspect of our life, the more we water and feed that plant. When you invest a lot of time and energy into something, you're growing a large plant.

"This can be amazing as we grow areas of our life to be big and beautiful. It can also be bad, if we spend too much time and effort in one area, or in areas that aren't healthy outlets. Some activities waste a lot of time, especially if they don't bring lasting joy and fulfillment.

Yet many people are building and watering their time garden, spending time on plants that don't give back. Instead of growing plants that create further joy and enlightenment. It's different for everyone, but some universal examples of smart investments are family, friends, nature, exercise, free thinking, writing, art, and more.

"At the time, Jade asked me, what kind of plants do you have in your garden? She was so worried about the plants in her garden. Even the ones from many years ago, the plants that represented her lack of productivity. I kept telling her to not dwell on the past, to focus on the future, to help others.

"Ever since Jade told me about the time garden, it has vexed me here and there as I review my own life. What kind of plants am I feeding and watering? What kind of garden am I cultivating? What kind of person am I becoming with my time? Is it time well-spent?" Ezra sighed and trailed off.

David cleared his throat and said, "Well, I know for myself, that you have a new plant in your garden. A plant named David. Everything I do, going forward, is affected by the time you gave me, by the time you dedicated to me when you didn't have to. You help people all the time, I think, by teaching the 5 Keys To Greatness, by spreading these ideas to others. Any time you want to contemplate the plants in your garden, you need to remember that."

Ezra laughed. "Fair enough." He put his water down. "Hmm. I've heard of a saying in the Talmud, from ancient rabbinical scholars, that says 'he who saves one life, it is as if he saved an entire world.' That must be what it's talking about–by saving someone, you create entirely new worlds through all their future actions."

Regina looked at David again. "I'm sorry. I don't want you to lose out because we're dealing with this." Regina closed her eyes, taking a deep breath. "You are basically all set. Apply the five keys to your life, using passion and action to infuse possibility into everything you do. You'll bring blessing into your life, so it can overflow into the lives of all those around you."

"Hear, hear," said Ezra, tilting his water bottle toward them.

"One more thing," Regina continued, "please send people our way. The first key is to Give, to provide for others. People everywhere can benefit from this framework. But they won't know about this system unless people like you share it. You need to give this to others, so they can elevate their own life, and then share it with others."

David laughed. "I just told my doctor about the 5 Keys. Remember Dr. Monaghan, Regina? The neurologist?"

Regina nodded and said, "That's amazing! That's what we need; we need your help to spread the 5 Keys To Greatness, so we can continue what we do. When you tell the people you care about to visit us, to learn from us, we can create the change we so desperately need in this world."

"I had a hunch about Dr. Monaghan. For the future, how can I tell who is right for the 5 Keys?" David asked.

"You'll know when people are ripe for a change. You can usually tell when someone is so frazzled that they need to hear a new solution to move forward. Young or old, together we can bring others to the point where we are all able to transcend everything around us.

"Imagine a new world. A world where everyone is giving, living a purpose-driven life, fully engaged in the moment, seeing the positive in every situation, and working tenaciously to achieve their goals. We'd transform the world into a wonderful place, by creating a new reality each and every day.

"All you have to do is send others our way. Tell people about the 5 Keys To Greatness, to visit me and my friends. You could even take over Jade's position as the one who explains tenacity."

David laughed nervously. "I don't know. I've never done an endurance event. I don't know when I was persistent to the point that I can be the role model for this."

Regina and Ezra chuckled while exchanging a look. "We all started off saying things like that. You have far more value to provide than you think. The first thing to remember is that you can almost always do enough to help people."

Regina fiddled with the beer tops as she said, "Every single person who has learned about the 5 Keys To Greatness is another person who can help. The more people who find their way to these life-changing keys, the better. This helps everyone, as you give back and help others find their own true path of greatness."

David nodded. "I can do that at least."

Regina laughed. "But if you want to be our keyholder for the fifth key, you'd be surprised at how well you could continue Jade's legacy. You have the power within you. Even if you only took people into the woods, showed them the hole in the rock, and told people about Jade, it would be enough. That alone would teach people about tenacity.

"You can let me know later, I won't push you for an answer now. Unless you want me to." Regina grinned.

"By the way, if you meet people who are lacking in self-esteem, be aware. They can learn about the 5 Keys To Greatness, but they will need to address their deep deficit in self-esteem. I'm not talking about someone who needs a little confidence, who can focus on a few ideas and be fine. I mean someone who needs, an intervention to improve their self-esteem. The same goes for personal confidence. You need it to move forward."

Regina sat back, beer in hand, and took a sip. David sat there, Ezra as well, as they shared a quiet moment. They reflected on life, on the five keys, on Jade. They thought about spending more time cultivating the important things in life, while letting everything else alone. Dusk settled into darkness. There was more quiet, more conversation, centered around Jade and her unstoppable optimism. After some time, David put his empty beer down. "I have to go soon."

The moon shone in the distance, brightening the darkness. Ezra leaned his head back on the chair, closed his eyes, and sighed.

Regina watched Ezra, then looked at David. "Understandable. Just remember to bring your best self to everything you do. The 5 Keys To Greatness are focused around you. Take personal responsibility for your own life, for the things that happen. It gives you the freedom to make things better. As we get better at taking responsibility and building on each key, we elevate our life and our interactions. Everything we have and experience is integrated into how we feel and interpret the world.

"I saw something fascinating the other day. A

psychologist, Dr. Alia Crum, did research while a student at Harvard. She tested how mindset affects our world, using different experiments to see how what we believe changes what we experience.

"I'll tell you about one of her experiments. She worked with women who were housekeepers for hotels. Same women, same job they always did, but for the experiment she split them into two groups. Half of the women watched a presentation describing the health benefits of their job. It showed them how doing their job was actually great exercise. For the others, they put up a poster in their break room about the health benefits of exercise.

"The housekeepers who did not get the presentation had virtually no changes. But the women who watched the presentation had improvements in every health metric; better blood pressure, better cholesterol, lower weight, and more. The presentation was only fifteen minutes! A short intervention gave them a different mindset about their job, and created amazing changes. They were doing the exact same job as before. They unlocked all of the benefits of a workout simply by believing it was great exercise.

"This experiment and many others continue to show that your mindset dictates your reality. What you think, what you believe about the world, will literally make your world.

"The 5 Keys To Greatness center around this principle. When you spend your time giving, focusing on your reason for living, engaging with your world, recognizing the amazing things about life, and staying tenacious in the face of adversity, you create a new reality. If it doesn't come naturally, you can create your own little intervention. Sit down and create a new reality for yourself by doing things like writing about your experiences. Or you can meditate your way into a new mindset." Regina sat back as she ran out of steam. "What I'm trying to say is that by focusing on living your best life, everything else will follow.

"We're here for you if you need us. We love helping people you send our way, and there is a place on our team when you are ready. You can be a keyholder. You can help us spread this message, continue Jade's legacy. If you want."

David nodded, and agreed to think about it. He stood to go. Regina and Ezra said their goodbyes, reminding David once more to share the 5 Keys To Greatness, so everyone can unlock their own best life.

13

Reflection at the Cliffs

D AVID PARKED HIS car, reflecting on how much had changed since he had last been at this spot only two weeks ago. He got out of the car and hiked up the trail to the cliff.

David walked through the trees, stepping on rocks, roots, gravel as he made his way up the hill. Back to the place where it all started. He thought of how different his life was already, as he started to implement each of the 5 Keys To Greatness. He focused on the trail in front of him, maintaining his mental presence. David thought of all the ways the 5 Keys To Greatness had brought him great wealth in the last two weeks. Not material wealth. Wealth in more satisfaction with what he had, wealth in more focus on the present moment, wealth in more awareness of ways he could give to others.

David reached the top, and sat down in almost the same spot as before. He kept thinking through what he learned. How the 5 Keys To Greatness integrated smoothly into his life, with the things he was doing. David sat, silent and alone, watching the cars fly by on the highway below.

"How's the view?" came a voice from behind David.

He turned, saw it was the same old man who helped him to begin with. David scrambled up and walked over to the man. "Pinch. Hey! How are you?"

Pinch shook David's hand in greeting, then waved off his offers to help him. "I'm good. More importantly, how are you?"

David nodded, then said, "I'm–I'm great. Better than I've been in a long time. I learned all about the 5 Keys To Greatness you told me about. They've improved my life in ways unimaginable."

Pinch nodded as he walked to the cliff and sat down where he sat that night. David walked over and sat back down too.

David continued, "I've already told a few people about the 5 Keys. I think it will change their lives."

Pinch smiled. "Sounds about right. What most people need is a little push in the right direction. They can usually handle everything else themselves. There are always those people who need more, but they need more help whether we try to help them or not.

"Have you ever heard that quote from Albert Einstein? 'Great spirits have always encountered violent opposition from mediocre minds.' Someone may be unable or unwilling to grab ahold of their own potential greatness. Or they may have underlying issues. Either way, focus on the people you can help. Don't let the people you can't help get to you."

"Yeah, I guess so."

The moment grew silent. The cars continued to fly by, always rushing to places unknown.

"Have you thought about how to put the 5 Keys To Greatness into practice? Any questions about it?" Pinch asked.

"Well, it's a lot. Sometimes I think about the people I know, how they've built themselves into a success. Then I think how much farther I have to go to get there. When I think of that, it makes me overwhelmed and exasperated."

"That makes perfect sense."

"It does?"

"Yes. Any time we compare our life to another person, in the sense of 'I wish I was there, not here,' it will create feelings of inadequacy and more. You are you. Regina is Regina. You can't compare your life to hers, or to anyone else, because you didn't live the same life. You didn't go through the same challenges.

"You will always have a different outcome. Even if you went through the exact same obstacles as someone else, you are a different person. Those same situations would bring you to an entirely different place, perhaps worse, perhaps better.

"In regard to trying to accomplish so much in so little time. Think about how the world actually works. Think about how people actually change. Nobody changes overnight. It is a gradual process. Just think about your friends, the people you know. Have you ever had any old friends you haven't seen in a long time, and then you see them again? When it's been a decade or so since you've last seen him or her?"

David thought about it. "Yes, I have friends like that, friends from high school. Why?"

"Did you notice that the person you remember is not the person you met up with again later? That he or she is vastly different?"

"Yes, I did. I never thought Kevin would be capable of doing the things he did, since I saw him last. Law school, marriage, kids, responsibility, just wow. The last time I saw him, he was a total screw up, goofing off all day long with zero ambitions. Actually, the last time I saw him was by some concert. He was a groupie, following them around. Now he's a respectable member of society, or so it seems."

"Exactly. You look at what he's done in five, ten, fifteen years, since you saw him last, and it's amazing. How could he do all of this!? How could he have made such a drastic transformation?

"Do you think that the transformation as he experienced it was drastic?"

David thought for a moment. "No, I suppose it was gradual, bit by bit."

"Gradual. Bit by bit. You said it, not me. This is how people change. One small decision after another, taken in totality, creates a vastly different life for the person. A little here, a little there, and they find themselves in an entirely different place.

"It is all about realigning, not on drastic, overnight change. If you try to jump straight into a new reality, you will never get there. Even if you get there, you will never be able to stay there. It takes slow and steady movement to get anywhere of substance.

"I like to use a parable of driving for this concept of realigning. Let's say you are driving on a major interstate, the I-80, and you are heading west. Then you realize that you really need to be on the I-90. What do you do? You can't jump from one highway to another. You can't transport your car to the new highway!

"You need to look at a map. You need to navigate a route to get from where you are to where you need to be. You can take a sharp turn and head only toward the new highway. This stops your forward progress until you are where you want to be. But if you navigate a diagonal path, your forward progress continues while you are realigning with the new highway.

"It's the same in life. You cannot magically change overnight. You can't jump yourself into a new way of living. You need to have a good idea of who you are and where you are. Have a decent idea of who you want to be, where you want to go. Only then can you navigate a path to get to the new you. And that path is traveled by moving slowly, taking one small step at a time.

"Focus on incremental improvement, on being better than you were yesterday. Then you can unlock the power of your own greatness, as you launch yourself to new heights. If you think back on your own life, you'll see that the times you achieved in leaps and bounds were the times that you took it one step at a time. When you focus on each next step, or on each goal and the steps you need to take to get there, slowly but surely hardships melt away. You're able to do it because when you take it one step at a time, it's easy. When you know the goal, it's much easier to take small steps to get there."

David thought about this, recognizing the truth in incremental improvement. The cars continued rushing by, as the daylight faded. David realized they would once again find their way down in the dark.

"Did anyone discuss balance with you?"

David nodded. "Celia talked about it."

"Good. You must balance your life to achieve anything. You've got to work on a mind-body-soul triangle of balance. The triangle is one of the strongest structures in building. As long as it is properly balanced. The second one side of the triangle is weaker than the others, the structure will collapse.

"You are not a building. So strengthening one side at a time won't cause you to collapse." They laughed. "The point is that you should try to work on all five keys as equally as possible. Maybe work a little on all five each day, or maybe focus on one key each week."

David nodded. "I've thought about that. I'm thinking about the best way to do it for me."

"Remember, David, that you can pick one way and change it later. You should always use whatever methods are working best for you. This will help you get the best possible results over the longest period of time. Being honest with yourself about what is and isn't working can be one of your greatest gifts, if you can achieve it.

"Have you thought about how you can put the 5

Keys To Greatness into action in your own life?"

David sat back, leaning on his hands. "A little. I think for now I will gain the most value by focusing on my personal and family life. I'm sure that the work I do in my personal life will overflow into my work life. But for now I need to concentrate on my personal life. Have you found something in particular that works the best?"

Pinch shook his head. "No. Not really. Each person is so different. Do what works best for you. Whatever you are thinking of doing, I urge you to start. Get to it. Sometimes contemplating how you will do something will stop you from ever doing it.

"Get low-tech, get simple. Grab a cheap notebook and start jotting down ideas. Journal a little each day, describing what you tried, and if it worked. Write up when you will work on each key, then keep to it. Above all, keep it simple. Don't allow anything like analysis paralysis to set in. Then you will have no forward progress, and that would be the biggest shame."

David nodded.

"Above all, remember that the 5 Keys To Greatness are about you. These are about elevating yourself, not the people around you. Don't worry how the people around you are acting. Don't worry how they are working, or thinking, or anything. The 5 Keys To Greatness is an internal program, it is a framework to help you connect to more of you.

"You can tell them about the system, if it seems right. And yes, there are many aspects of the 5 Keys that will overflow onto the people in your life. But focus on yourself. This is a framework to help you build a connection to yourself, to live your own best life."

The moon began to peek over the trees, the last of the sunlight disappearing. The moon was large, glowing, yellow, nearly full. The type of moon you expect to see shining over miracles.

Pinch laughed. "I could go on about this all night if you let me. But I'm running out of time, and I think you need to be getting back soon as well.

"I do want to tell you one or two more things though, before we trek back down.

"Your thoughts are all powerful. The more you fixate on something, the more you can change the world. Both for the good and the bad. There is a saying in the Talmud, talking about how we end up doing things we sometimes never meant to do. It says, 'the eye sees, the mind thinks, the heart desires, the body does,' or close enough to that. The more that we look and think, the more likely it is that we will end up doing it. Yes, this applies to things we shouldn't be doing, but I think it also applies to good things. If you want to actualize something, you need to be obsessed. You need to see, think, desire, and do. It takes this obsession to bring something from the world of thought into the world of action.

"Have you noticed that we live in two distinct worlds? The world of thought and the world of action. Our thoughts and desires, wants and needs go forever unfulfilled in the world of our mind. We think, ruminate, calculate and more, but it all stays in our mind. Some things, those we want badly enough, or fear badly enough, move from the world of our thoughts into the world we live in. They move into this world of actions, the world of deeds.

"Sometimes when those thoughts become actions, it is a good thing; other times, it is a bad thing. I want to point this out to you. I want you to make sure that the things you bring from your world of thought to our world of action are good things.

"There is an ancient Chinese proverb, with a similar theme. 'Be careful of your thoughts, for your thoughts become your words. Be careful of your words, for your words become your actions. Be careful of your actions, for your actions become your habits. Be careful of your habits, for your habits become your character. Be careful of your character, for your character becomes your destiny.'

"So I implore you: Go. Fly. Find your thoughts. Find your words. Find your actions. Find your habits.

Find your destiny." The older man exhaled, with a sense of finality hard to break.

David sensed that this was it, that there would be no more, no more to learn. No longer a time for learning, now a time for action. Now a time to use passion and action to apply the 5 Keys To Greatness to his life. The time was nigh. David felt it, palpable.

David felt the invitation in the wind, in the night sky, in the rushing cars below, in the glowing moon above. It seemed as if the whole universe was rooting for him at that moment. Asking him to do it. Asking him to take action.

Epilogue

Farewell to Pinch

D AVID AND PINCH got up a short time later. They carefully walked down the path together, using dim flashlights and the bright moonlight. They talked on the way down, but the conversation had long since moved on from the 5 Keys To Greatness.

As they walked down the trail, they were able to see every rock, every root, despite the darkness apparent.

David recalled a time he was on a hike that went past sunset. He was surprised how well his group could see using only the flashlight on the back of his phone and the moon. It is amazing that in total darkness only a little light is needed to see the way.

Fortunately, the walk wasn't long. There may be trails that meander for miles to reach an overlook, but this wasn't one of them.

As the trees thinned, David saw his car ahead. He trailed off as he walked the last little bit. When he could see his entire car, he stopped and turned to Pinch. "Pinch, thank you. I can't tell you how much this means to me. How much this means to my family. They may never realize how amazing this has been. But this has been life-changing, to say the least."

Pinch stood there, smiling. He looked down, looked back up at David, with soft eyes. He nodded, slowly, imperceptibly. "Don't worry. I know. I'm happy I was here in the right place, at the right time, for you."

David glanced down, reached in his pocket, grabbed his keys.

Pinch went on. "I don't get to visit much anymore. So I don't get to help people like I used to. But there are certain people, certain souls, for whom I can still intercede. I'm still able to help them. I am proud, and honored, to have been a part of your life."

David laughed. "You sound like I won't see you again." Pinch smiled. David looked at his car again, noticing there was no other car around. "Hey, where did you park? Do you need help getting to your–" David turned back to Pinch, but there was no longer anyone there.

"Pinch?"

David felt goosebumps raising on his arms, on the back of his neck. He took a step forward. "Pinch?!"

The stars twinkled. The moon shone brightly down. David looked around, realizing the path had lost its illumination, had lost the clarity from moments before. He looked at his flashlight, to be sure it was still on; it was.

David thought again about what he noticed before. In total darkness, only a little light is needed to see the way. Time to create a little light to chase away the darkness.

He called one more time, now in a whisper, in disbelief, "Pinch?"

David could feel the whisper of his own name playing in the wind that flowed through the trees, in the wind that seemed to play the song of the world. It soothed his very breath. He stood there, in the moment, taking a few minutes before traveling home to his wife and his family. Eyes closed, he reveled in the strange heady feeling. The breeze whistled through the trees. The chirps and songs played the nighttime symphony of the forest. The cars whooshed by, the noise barely perceptible from the highway. He let it all, everything, wash over him. Destiny awaits.

About the Author

ARI GUNZBURG IS is a rising new star in the world of personal growth. As an award-winning international speaker, and now writer, Ari uses storytelling and more to  bring life to inspiring ideas. Ari motivates audiences everywhere with his energizing delivery, raw, emotional style, and personal stories filled with triumph and travail, tragedy and transformation. As a dynamic conference keynote speaker and seminar presenter, and now virtual presenter, Ari speaks to people to spark a little light in a sea of darkness.

At only ten years old, Ari's teacher passed away

while on a hiking trip with the class. That moment changed Ari's life and perspective forever. Following the death of his teacher, there was a domino effect of changes and decisions, culminating in Ari getting his "PhD" from the school of hard knocks.

Ari's teenage years led him through life experiences uncommon to many, making Ari an authority in perseverance, maintaining a positive outlook, and embracing change and challenge. Ari brings this wisdom to the stage as he delivers thoughts on change, greatness, leadership, and more for corporations, associations, educational institutions, prisons, and more.

Now Ari is the founder of MindSpark, a company devoted to spreading messages of hope and change to people interested in personal development. He is the author of 4 beloved children's books, with more on the way, giving hope to children and parents everywhere.

Ari lives in Maryland with his wife and four children. He enjoys nature, hiking, rock climbing, cycling, reading, spending time with his wife and kids, and more.

Acknowledgements

FIRST AND FOREMOST, thank you to God. For placing me in this world, in my circumstances, for everything I've been given, and for everything withheld as well. It is all for the best. Thank you.

Thank you to my wife, for being there at all times, no matter how deeply I fall into a project. Words cannot describe my appreciation adequately. Thank you, for everything, and all. For forever and a day.

Thank you to my wonderful children, whose exuberance is both distracting and refreshing at the same time. Thank you for your bright eyes, your laughable comments, and all of the life that you bring into our home.

Thank you to my parents, for everything. It's been a

wild ride, and yet we are still here, still talking, which may be a miracle in and of itself. I know I've been difficult at times, and for that I'm sorry. A special thank you to my father, whose command of grammar and rhythm helped shape this book.

Thank you to my Rebbe, Rabbi Mandelbaum. Your light and your guidance will be with me always, though you were taken away from us prematurely.

A special thank you to Jack Honig, for his timely efforts to ensure there are no errors in this book. Any errors after his reading are surely my own (please let me know if you see something so I can fix it). Speaking of errors, much of what happens with the doctor in this story is likely inaccurate, as I fabricated it to suit the story.

Thank you to my first round of readers. Your advice, or the lack thereof, helped me see where I could improve this book, where I could tighten up the corners. To others who helped proofread this story, thank you.

A special thank you and my deep appreciation to Sara Hawkins, who checked every word and called me out on my redundancies and helped add color and variance to this book.

Thank you to my larger family. From siblings, to in-laws, to siblings in-law, to all of my nieces and nephews. All of you are a part of what makes me, me. A specific thank you to my brother and brother-in-law who are always available for advice.

And a special thank you to my mother-in-law, who defines what giving truly means. From her constant calls, to her consistent care that we have all we need, I couldn't have asked for a better mother-in-law. Additionally, I got the inspiration for this book while working a job I got through her connections. Thank you to the K's as well; I meant to write a different book that summer, but instead I discovered the 5 Keys To Greatness.

Thank you to Rabbi Akiva, who is the inspiration for the hole in the stone. Rabbi Akiva lived this story over 2000 years ago. At forty years old, at the behest of his wife, he went to learn in the rabbinical academy. He was illiterate and unknowledgeable, not even knowing his letters. Rabbi Akiva left the academy, because it was too hard. He thought he couldn't make it. On his way home, he sat down by a rock, which had a hole in it, created by the steady dripping of water. He deduced that if water, which is soft, can make a hole in rock, which is hard, by being persistent, then how much more so could he gain the knowledge he dreamed of, by being persistent.

Thank you to Les Brown; you don't know me, but your motivational speeches are a large part of what got me started on this journey. And while I'm thanking people who got me started on this journey, thank you to CP and her boys. It was through agreeing to come speak to your boys, the young men incarcerated in Cuyahoga County, and the encouragement they gave me, that I started out as a speaker. Thank you.

Thank you to all of the scientists, writers, pioneers and more who are mentioned throughout this book. Your work, your words, have been influential in my life. I hope your ideas continue to inspire people the world over, through this book and others.

Thank you to Ezra, Kai, Leia, and my team for their constant support and strength. Thank you to Racquel Isaacs, for her help with the 5 Keys To Greatness videos, which should be out by the end of 2020.

Lastly, and again, I want to say thank you to God. Without you, there is nothing. It wasn't, and then it was. Thank you, for making it be.

The 5 Keys To Greatness

P ASSION AND ACTION help unlock every key of the 5 Keys To Greatness. Both help; if you have one and not the other, you won't get anywhere. You can be passionate, but if you never take action, you won't achieve anything. You can take action all the time, but without passion, it will be hard to stay the course. Passion and action help you maintain your forward momentum.

The word to remember the 5 Keys To Greatness is GREAT.

Give.

Reason.

Engage.

Amazing.

Tenacity.

And now a short explanation of each key.

*   *   *

GIVE - one of the greatest joys in life is giving. By focusing on being more selfless, you can expand your life in ways never thought possible.

REASON - having a purpose in life gives you drive and direction. It also helps you be happier. As you strive to achieve that purpose, you create meaning in your entire life.

ENGAGE - humans are social creatures. If you don't participate in the things around you, you will be alienated. If you aren't fully present at the moments in your life, you'll miss out on your own life. Your social connections help you feel fulfilled.

AMAZING - mindset is everything. By shifting your mindset, by applying a positive mindset to your circumstances, you shift your entire life.

TENACITY - keep the end in mind and persevere to achieve your goals. "Seven times a righteous man falls and yet he rises again," said King Solomon in Proverbs. Get up and back out there no matter what happens. Persistence helps you achieve the greatness within you.

*   *   *

That is the 5 Keys To Greatness. Use these five focal points in your own life, make them mean whatever makes the most sense to you. Own them. Launch yourself on your own way to greatness.

Above all, remember to give the 5 Keys To Greatness to others. You can tell people there is a free download on the website, 5KeysToGreatness.com. It describes all five keys. Anyone can have it, use it, internalize it, and create their best life with it.

Share it with others, so we may all continue on our way to greatness.

-Ari Gunzburg

P.S. On the next page is a chart for you to hang up or use anywhere you like.

Give *provide*

Reason *purpose*

Engage *presence*

Amazing *positivity*

Tenacity *persistence*

5 KEYS TO GREATNESS

More About the 5 Keys

THERE IS MORE to learn if you want! Each product is designed to be used on its own or in conjunction with the other programs. It is entirely your choice. The methods of presenting and the examples used are different in each program, to give you a fresh new way of looking at the materials.

To learn more about the 5 Keys To Greatness using other available products such as the video presentation, the workbook, and the online forum, please visit the website 5KeysToGreatness.com.

A Simple Request

I WOULD LOVE to hear your thoughts. Please send me your stories! Or answer any or all of these questions.

- What have you learned from this book?
- How have the 5 Keys To Greatness had a positive effect on your life?
- What did you think of the book?
- How has this book changed your life for the better?
- Do you have any additional thoughts or insights?

I'll do my best to reply with a personal note.

-Ari

Please use this form to send your thoughts:
5KeysToGreatness.com/thoughts

Children's Books by Ari Gunzburg

Someday Soon

While our current situation with Covid19 is difficult, our youngest children are wondering, will it ever end? This hopeful book brings up many things a small child may want to do, then reminds him or her that someday soon, things will go back to normal.

Coronavirus Brave

With school starting in 2020 in a modified format all over, parents are making personal decisions about how to send their kids to school. Many kids are wondering how it will all work. This book gives hope back to children, and reminds them that together, we can all be coronavirus brave.

Nobody Cares

This delightful book rhymes and shines its way to a special place in your child's heart. Learn to be more comfortable being yourself, because, after all, nobody cares.

Cheese Monsters

Romp around with friendly cheesy monsters on their way to bed. This is a story told in verse of kids who love cheese. They amuse their father while running the show and creating a big mess! There is a surprise ending with the appearance of a final monster. And then the kids are put to bed, making this a great book to use to put your kids to bed.

Available on Amazon.

Free Offer

Want to discuss ideas and ways to implement the 5 Keys To Greatness? Describe what works best for you, learn what others have done, which other systems fit?

Join the soon-to-be-launched online forum! Go to the website, 5KeysToGreatness.com and sign up for the mailing list. When the forum launches, you will receive an early invitation to join, at no cost.

The goal of the forum is to bring keyholders together so that everyone can gain. From giving back to others who are finding their way through the journey to getting help from others, together everyone on the forum can work together to unlock the greatness within.

Go to **5KeysToGreatness.com** today and sign up for the mailing list! Together we can work to achieve our destiny.

Printed in Poland
by Amazon Fulfillment
Poland Sp. z o.o., Wrocław